THE
PITIFUL
GARDENER'S
HANDBOOK

THE
PITIFUL GARDENER'S
HANDBOOK

• Successful Gardening •
In Spite   of Yourself

Connie Eden & Tracy Cheney

The Pitiful Gardener Handbook
© 1999 by Connie Eden and Tracy Cheney

ISBN 1-881409-23-6
Cover and book design: Marge Mueller, Gray Mouse Graphics
Illustrations: Tracy Cheney
Production, typesetting, and layout: Marge Mueller, Gray Mouse
    Graphics

JASI   P.O. Box 313
       Medina, Washington 98039
       (425)454-3490; fax: (425)462-1335;
       e-mail: jasibooks@aol.com

Printed in the United States of America

Library of Congress Cataloging-in-Publication Data

Eden, Connie, 1955–
    The pitiful gardener's handbook : successful gardening, in spite of
yourself / Connie Eden & Tracy Cheney.
       p. cm.
    ISBN 1-881409-23-6 (pbk.)
    1. Gardening Handbooks, manuals, etc. I. Cheney, Tracy, 1956–.
    II. Title.
SB450.96.E386 1999
635.9—dc21   99-25415
                                                       CIP

❧ DEDICATION ❧

To Bob and Bill for taking care of the kids and us. To Drew, Brynn, and Lauren for letting us get our work done. You're the best! Books don't get written without that kind of support.

——*Love, C. E. and T.W.C.*

Contents

EPILOG

PITIFUL NO MORE   153

APPENDICES   155

INDEX   173

It's Not a Garden Without You

God doesn't garden. Neither does Mother Nature. Human beings garden.

Gardening begins and ends with people. Gardens don't just happen on their own; they have to be created by someone who takes natural things and mixes them up unnaturally. On the surface, gardening appears to be a wholly natural act. After all, we're dealing with plants, dirt, water, and air, and they're all natural. However, gardening is really the act of manipulating the plant environment around your house in a different way than what occurs naturally. Depending on what you want your garden to look like, sometimes you work with the natural processes and sometimes you work against them.

Humans aren't born knowing how to do this. Even so, if you've ever planted anything in your yard, you're already involved. Folks who have figured it out are called gardeners. Others—who are somewhere in the middle of the process and don't yet understand it fully—may come to the conclusion that they're stuck with a brown thumb forever. If you think you fall into this second category, then *The Pitiful Gardener's Handbook* is for you.

We are constantly bombarded by images of the "perfect" or "ideal" garden in magazine pictures at the checkout stand. But are these gardens even attainable by the average busy person? Is it like striving for the sleek model's body and then feeling as if you've fallen short? The thing is, there isn't one desirable look, as gardening can go off in so many different directions. But it's not always easy to have realistic gardening aspirations that are in line with the amount of time we want to spend in our yards, especially when the professionals make it look so appealing. With the proliferation of gardening information, it seems as if humans have to know a lot to be successful, but you really only have to know enough to make your own garden work for you.

This book gives you the big picture of gardening that underlies the kind of knowledge gardeners gain intuitively from spending time in their yards over many years. When it comes to deciding how much you want to participate in the manipulation of nature, it helps to understand how and why things fit together. You don't even have to particularly like gardening to be successful. The goal is to create the kind of garden that best suits your interest and knowledge level at any given time.

The Pitiful Gardener's Handbook shows you what Mother Nature and humans do in the garden and who's responsible for what. This knowledge will help you maximize whatever you're currently doing, and help you choose suitable plants in the future. The *Handbook* is designed to help you figure out the difference between what you imagine you'd like to have and what you realistically can accomplish in your garden. The focus is on you first, and your garden second. You will learn to be in control of your garden, rather than your garden in control of you.

PART ONE

What Is a Garden?

The dictionary defines "garden" as a "plot of ground where herbs, fruits, flowers or vegetables are *cultivated*." So, then, a garden is a place where someone has gathered together a collection of plants and tends them with tools. It isn't a garden without the assortment of plants or the use of tools. And it is the domain of humans, made for human purposes. A garden is much too narrow to contain the enormous systems of Mother Nature. She has a much different agenda.

WHY YOU'D NEVER WANT MOTHER NATURE AS YOUR GARDENER

Mother Nature is the ultimate artist, with the earth as her canvas. Climate, topography, and the complete spectrum of flora and fauna are her palette. The resulting works of art are entire regions—prairies, steppes, alpine regions, redwood forests. Such places are not just collections of plants, but complete ecosystems of flora and fauna that have evolved together through time. Mother Nature has the knack for placing plants in the right spot so that they fulfill their destinies—the continuation of their species.

Mother Nature isn't in the gardening business because she doesn't tend to things delicately. The "tools" that shape the landscape, such as floods and hurricanes, are broad in scope and often wreak havoc in a garden. A drought season may kill even the hardiest of natives. Rain pelts tough plants, as well as the tender ones. Hail splits leaves indiscriminately. Winds rip off branches, but rarely the ones you wanted pruned.

While gardening isn't Mother Nature's business, the natural succession of species is. The grand scheme in the wild dictates that one group of plants provides nutrients and shelter for the next group coming up in an unrelenting evolution of change and growth. This is the opposite of what the gardener desires to happen in the yard. Most gardeners want plants to remain fixed at a certain point in their development. Trying to choke off evolution, while keeping everything alive at the same time, goes against the natural cycle of the very plants the gardener has chosen. That's where managing and maintaining a garden comes in. An untended garden soon reverts to what's native to the region. "Weeds" move in, trees will sprout. A forest or prairie is natural, a garden is not. No matter how much we change the flora, Mother Nature continually vies with us to return the landscape to a more original state.

Gardeners have at their disposal Mother Nature's immense palette, but select just a bit of what's available. Since the plants and elements used to create the garden don't originate with humans, it isn't possible to change the larger scheme of how they were originally intended to work together. The goal is to duplicate their growing conditions to some degree and combine the various plant choices into workable relationships in the smaller scale of your yard.

MOTHER NATURE'S THREE PRINCIPLES

Although a garden is a human creation, you don't actually control it. There are too many forces beyond any gardener's command affecting the garden. The ultimate control of the garden always lies with Mother Nature, so you will make your garden experience most successful by abiding by Mother Nature's three fundamental principles.

The first principle is to accept "what is." Essentially, this means accepting that there are natural plant characteristics you just can't change. It means acknowledging that each species of tree has its own mature height and shape—and then giving it adequate space to do what it's going to do. Wanting to control the tree's height or shape will cause you to cut it back frequently. You create more work (and problems) for yourself whenever you buck a plant's normal growth pattern. Each one follows its own particular cycle that you can only tweak, not control. You can't make it become something else or do anything it doesn't have a natural inclination to do. Without an awful lot of hard work on your part, a plant is always going to try to be what it is naturally meant to be, period.

The second principle to keep in mind is that all plants have three basic needs—sun, water, and soil. They're all the same in that respect; the difference lies in the way the amounts of these elements are individually combined for each plant. Each one has specific needs in order to flourish, and you must provide what it requires.

The third principle always at work is that time brings change. Nothing on the planet remains static, including plants. While time is not much of a factor in altering your handiwork on the inside of your home, it is a continual one in your yard. Time makes the word "garden" a verb as well as a noun, because humans have to actively respond to its effects. Plants are four-dimensional. You work with the three dimensional elements of height, width, and depth, plus the additional factor of time, or continual growth.

You also deal with time in the life cycles of plants. Since plants grow at different rates, knowing how quickly something will reach its mature height helps determine where to put it in the first place. Trees are the only plants that are really long-lived. The other species will die off at different intervals. Plants never stay the same, even though you might like them to stop at the point where you think it's all perfect. There is a strong human tendency to try to override Mother Nature's schedule in the multifaceted place we call the garden.

- 18 -

ANATOMY OF A GARDEN

A garden functions on multiple levels at the same time. It is simultaneously a unique place, a process, and a community within a community. A garden represents the choices that the gardener makes, as well as the personal taste that produces the visual and emotional experience of that particular space. Every garden is similar in the sense that the first three (place, process, and community) are present to some degree. But every garden is different because of the choices and preferences of the individual gardener.

A garden is a unique place

A garden is a subjective experience and creation. Every garden means something different to its creator, and no two gardens can look just alike, even if you use the identical plants your neighbor uses. The numerous small decisions you make over time—whether or not to prune, how often to water—affect the outcome. Your garden is as personal as your handwriting. It is a spot where who you are, what you know or don't know about gardening, and what you're going to do or not do about it all come together.

Each garden site is unique as well, even within a neighborhood. The placement of buildings, trees, and fences on each lot produces variations of shade and sun patterns. Microclimates, such as little frost pockets, warm spots from reflected sunlight, or damp areas created from runoff, exist within a landscape. Even off-site influences affect your garden. Your neighbors' tall trees and buildings can shade and cool your landscape, and pests from your neighbors' plants as well as their weed seeds come floating over fences. Your responses to these factors help to make your garden individual.

A garden is a process

A garden is subject to relentless change—by its very nature it's active. It's different in the morning than in the evening, with altered shade patterns and temperature. It changes season to season, year to year. Plants continually grow and age. This process, visible in nature, becomes even more dramatic in a garden because the growing and aging rates vary wildly. The more complex the garden, the more dynamic it is. In addition, not only are the plants themselves growing, but the garden as a whole has a collective activity as well. It evolves quickly or slowly depending upon the plants you've combined together. It may seem as if change happens randomly, but it really is consistent with what you've put into place.

When you're starting a garden from scratch, you're putting things together that have different time clocks. When you buy a home with an established landscape, this variation can be even more pronounced. The plants are at different points of their life cycle; some may be on their way out, but you can't really know where they are in the process. Like all living things, they're aligned to Mother Nature's schedule.

A garden is always on its way to becoming something else. It's not a static object or place. Without your intervention it will always change. If you'd rather arrest your garden at a certain point of development, you'll find yourself more proactive than if you had left things to their own devices. Management issues kick in whenever you don't allow the garden to evolve unhindered in its own way and time. If you don't want Mother Nature as your gardener, then figure you're going to have to put something of yourself into the gardening process—even if it's just mowing the lawn and occasionally weeding.

A garden is a community within a community

No garden exists in isolation. A garden is always the product of a series of relationships both inside and outside of itself. The first relationship is between individual plants and the soil—and this is affected by where they are located in the yard. Then comes the relationship among all the plants themselves. Plants will be what they'll be, but they will be impacted by the relationships they're placed in— some overshadow shorter plants, some need more nutrients and deplete their neighbors' soil, some attract pests that feed on their neighbors, and some invite a host of fauna that might not otherwise come.

Every garden is also related to the larger environment outside it. Gardens are networked to each other by seed-carrying breezes, birds, and animals as well as by insects that may be either beneficial or destructive. Even once you've created your personal ecosystem and proceeded to get all the internal relationships working, it's still ultimately subject to the vagaries of climate in your region.

An important part of the gardening process is discovering not only the "connectedness" within your garden, but your connection to it. The most integral relationship of all exists between the garden and the gardener—whether it is all-consuming, neglectful, or somewhere between those extremes. You are an inherent part of the system. Your influence is embedded in the garden.

A garden reflects what the gardener knows

A garden represents an accumulation of choices, which may or may not have been based on knowledge. Many plants are put into the right place accidentally and do just fine. So, even though the garden is the outcome between theory and practice, it doesn't mean you have to know much to make it successful. However, gardening knowledge empowers you to bring about any changes you desire. And without the requisite knowledge, you waste time reacting to the consequences of what was destined to happen in the first place.

Gardening can seem simple or difficult, depending on what you've already experienced. We're commonly seduced by the notion that it's all easy because the gardening industry makes it seem as if anyone can garden with minimum effort or know-how. Attractive catalogs, seed packets, and magazine covers seem to suggest you could almost "plant-by-number" and have quick success. But a successful garden occurs with more certainty—independent of guesswork—only as you become knowledgeable about gardening and your specific yard and its conditions. That knowledge may even lead you to the realization that if your yard is ever to approximate your dream garden, you need to hire someone else to care for it.

As a gardener, you can acquire knowledge from many sources:

- Ask questions at the nursery or from more experienced gardeners.
- Read books and articles.
- Take workshops.
- Learn from trial and error in your own yard.
- Hire a garden designer to tell you specifically what to do.

The goal is to be in charge of the gardening choices you make so that your garden suits you. Your garden can be in tune with the surrounding ecosystem or in opposition to it. It can reflect organization or chaos. Either way, your garden will grow; the difference lies in the amount of work it will require of you.

A garden is personal

Gardening is a visual and emotional experience. It gives you visual feedback on the choices you've made. Sometimes you have to step back to *see* your landscape. Are you getting what you want from it? A garden isn't about agriculture. It exists only for your pleasure, even if it's just to serve as decoration around the foundation of your house. A garden is personal. It can't help but be so.

A garden is an emotional experience because the collection of plants in your garden was put together by an individual with certain gardening likes and dislikes—color, shape, plant preference—even if that person wasn't you. However, even if you didn't personally create your garden, a successful garden is still one that satisfies you. Whatever size or level of complexity your garden assumes shouldn't make you frustrated. Your ideal garden should satisfy you on a variety of levels:

- You have plants you know how to care for.
- You don't *have to* spend any more time gardening than you want to.
- You like the way it all looks.

Basically, the garden should be tailored to your needs. Part two of this book will show you how create that garden, while part three will tell you how to maintain it.

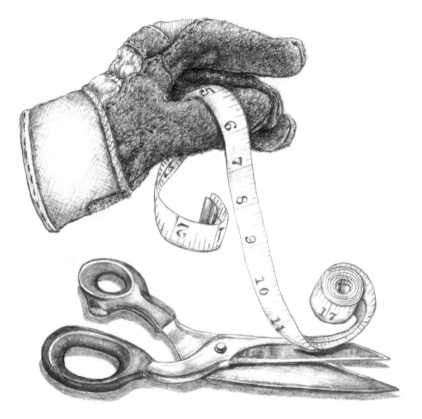

PART TWO

Tailoring Your Garden to Suit You

Outside your front door you're creating a personal eco-system with elements that are constantly growing, exfoliating, blooming, and crawling with life. This mini-ecosystem is unique to your property, existing nowhere else on the planet. You're the catalyst that makes it happen.

Humans play two roles in the garden: They bring it into existence, and then ensure that the garden remains in existence. That is, you not only create, but also manage your garden. Many of the plants in your yard wouldn't survive without your help. Your design won't remain intact without attention. Some parts of the design might live on without you—although in altered form—but a good portion would disappear.

Humans as garden creators

Your garden is for you. Making it work should include two considerations. The first consideration is your attitude about gardening, for it determines what you should have in it and how much. What do you want from your gardening experience? The second is the amount of time you can realistically devote to it over an extended length of time. Remember, a garden is a long term commitment.

How each garden is put together is as individual as the gardener. Mother Nature provides a huge smorgasbord of plants to pick and choose from, and you can base your choice of plants on a variety of criteria—or none at all! The criteria that drive the creation and eventual evolution of a garden can be fairly eclectic. One gardener may feel successful only when using the same plants over and over, while another may select plants that are easy to care for. Other criteria could be picking out whatever strikes one's fancy at the store, filling in a particular bare spot, collecting plants that attract certain animals or insects, recreating existing garden styles such as an English country garden or formal rose garden, or replicating existing systems such as a wetland or a native plant collection. There may be no other criteria than trying to find plants that you won't kill!

It's not often that you start out designing a garden from scratch. Usually you're refining or dramatically changing an existing landscape. You could be working around plants you inherited from the previous owner of your home. You may even have some plants that aren't entirely suitable in your garden, although sometimes this doesn't become apparent for a few years. Since plants can develop in so many different ways, if you don't have a lot of experience with a certain plant, it can be hard to imagine what it will become as it matures. As you make changes to your yard, the personal criteria you've developed—whether you're conscious of it or not—serve as your guide in plant selection.

Gardeners begin to feel pitiful when what they want their gardens to look like and what they're willing to work for are two different things. The garden that best suits you is determined by the amount and types of plants you put in it. While some plants are relatively carefree, others are high maintenance, demanding fairly constant attention. The real key to growing plants successfully is to have ones that match the way you garden. As you alter your style and the amount of time you spend in the garden, the palette of plants you choose from will expand or contract as well.

This section of the book shows how you can have it all—a garden that looks nice and that you're willing and able to care for without too much expertise. It's a personal journey to discover what works best for you.

Focusing your efforts in this way transforms you into an effective garden creator, because understanding yourself and your garden provides you a mental process we call "filters," through which you can make the best plant choices for you and your garden site.

FILTER FIRST, PLANT LATER

The first phase of Garden Tailoring is to create three mental filters. To discover what the parameters of your filters should be, you'll focus on your garden, yourself, and the plants you choose. These filters help you develop a personal plant list and bring order to your garden.

To help you create your three filters:

- Analyze your garden to build the *Site Filter*.
- Analyze yourself to put together your *Personal Filter*.
- Analyze your plant choices to compile your *Plant Filter*.

As you begin putting these together, you'll be thinking about your garden before you buy anything, thereby giving yourself a head start toward success. Many people buy on impulse and try to figure out what to do later. Using filters allows you to take control of how you'll interact with the garden (and the garden store).

Without filters in place, you can end up with a lovely garden, but it will probably take a good measure of trial and error to get there. Your other option is to hire a landscape designer to figure it all out for you.

Using filters also allows you to control the degree of simplicity or complexity in any flower bed. Complexity just means several things are going on at the same time around the garden. Call it "eye candy" because it's more of a visual thing—layers of plant heights, for instance. The more criteria you impose on a flower bed, the more elaborate it becomes. But this complexity doesn't necessarily mean a lot more work in the garden since you can choose extremely easy-care plants. Creating complexity is a mental exercise. The work comes in the planning stage.

What Do You Have? Build Your Site Filter

To construct your site filter you'll be assessing the physical conditions existing in your yard. You'll also note what you find pleasing in it, and what you want to fix or change. It may be that you're not interested in analyzing your garden right away, and that's fine. But eventually you've got to bite the bullet if garden tailoring is going to work for you. Start with a small area and keep it simple.

Choose One Bed (or Area) to Work On

Don't tackle the whole yard at once, and the first time you use this method, select an easy-care area. If you choose a bed that you pass through frequently (maybe one close to the front door or near a patio), you'll notice when things need to be tended and increase your odds for success.

Physical inventory

To get going, take stock of what's in this bed. Become familiar with its conditions and the factors influencing it. Consider what it is you have to work with and build from there.

Sun and Shade. If you're able to start in a place you know and understand well, you won't have to guess how much sun it gets during the day. Assessing the bed in the dormant season before trees have leafed out, however, doesn't give you an accurate picture of shade patterns or temperatures. You need to be familiar with conditions during the middle of summer. Then you'll know the most intense and stressful conditions you'll be subjecting the plants to during the growing season. It's important to note if your targeted bed sits out in the full sun without any shelter. If you've chosen a bed out in the back forty you'll need to keep track of it for a day. Note where the shade—if any—falls in the morning, at noon, and in the late afternoon.

Wind and Weather. Exposure to various weather-related elements can also determine a plant's chance for survival. You may have the right light conditions for some plants, but harsh winds or unrelenting heat could still knock them out of contention. Be aware of any influence that your house, neighboring buildings, outbuildings, large trees, fences, or hedges have on moderating temperatures and wind exposure.

Plants. While it's helpful to know what general categories of plants you've got, such as shrubs or trees, the really useful information comes from identifying what's thriving and what's expired. If you don't know their names, take a stem cutting (with a good example of the leaves and flowers, if possible) to a nursery. Take along any spent flowers or seed pods found beneath the plant. You'll then know exactly which families of plants did well in a particular spot and which to avoid.

Soil. The soil in your garden is one of the major factors determining the types of plants you'll be able to grow well. Use the quick "clump" test to figure out what kind of topsoil you've got. While it won't give you a complete diagnosis of your soil, it will give you a handle on your soil profile. Squeeze some soil in your hand. Pure sand slips through your fingers. Pure clay stays in a solid lump. If it clumps and holds its shape, yet breaks apart around the edges, it's loam. Loam can accommodate the widest variety of plants. Fortunately, the majority of people don't have the extremes of all sandy or all clay soils, which limit the kind of plants that can be grown in them. Most soils exist somewhere on a gradient between the two. If you still feel unsure about your soil, ask the staff at an area nursery. They tend to be gardeners themselves and know what soil types exist locally. (For more information on soils, see page 125–132.)

The Bed. Note the depth, width, and any height restrictions (is it under a tree, the eaves, or telephone wires?) to judge whether or not your garden can accommodate the mature sizes of the plants you're considering. Take into account the location of existing plants and any mediating environmental factors—fences, buildings, and trees.

Aesthetic inventory

Begin by looking at your entire yard. Are there areas you're proud of or receive compliments on? Consider duplicating or extending them. They might possess these qualities:

- A nice variety of plant types, shapes, and sizes

- A powerful, seasonal color statement—lots of plants blooming at the same time
- A place that is a pleasure to be in—maybe a sense of enclosure created by trees, shrubs, or vines
- A few strong focal points that stand out and draw your eyes to them
- A variety of foliage colors and sizes
- Paths and other hardscapes—such as patios, trellises, decks

THE DEAD, THE DYING, AND THE UGLY

Once you've figured out what's been successful in your yard, you're ready to apply this knowledge to your designated bed. But along with this, you also need to decide what was a bust so that you don't repeat it. Do you have any of the following detracting elements?

Dead plants. Is everything else in your neighborhood leafed out or in full bloom, but you've got one sorry plant just sitting there with bare branches? You don't have to wait until every plant in town has blossomed before you come to the realization that it might actually be dead, beyond hope of resuscitation. Dead is dead, no matter how long you wait.

You can verify a plant's demise for yourself in three ways:

1. *Branch color.* Dead branches are usually gray. If they're gray just at the tips, your plant may have suffered winter frost damage. Cut off the damaged wood.

2. *Elasticity.* Try gently bending a branch towards the ground. If the branch arches and has some elasticity, most likely it's still viable. If it's brittle and

snaps off easily, look at the interior. Dead branches will be brown or gray inside, showing no green. You can keep checking all the way down to the base of the branch or until you have found the end of the dieback.

3. *The scratch test.* With your fingernail, scratch off a little bit of bark on a suspicious branch. If there's a green layer between the bark and the woody interior, then it's alive. If it's brown—yep, it's dead.

Crowded plants. Two plants can grow into each other at the expense of one plant's health when an area has been overplanted or the size of mature plants wasn't visualized when they were installed. The problem first shows up when one of the two plants has diminished foliage or flowers. Look for dead branches where they intermingle. Most likely one is suffering more than the other, and eventually the less vigorous one will become ugly or die.

If there's dieback all the way to the center, you can deal with it in one of four ways:

1. *Ignore.* You may be able to let things go for a long time without doing anything if it doesn't really bother you.

2. *Pitch.* This is the time-efficient solution. Sometimes you just have to cut your losses and get on with things. If you do remove something, let the bare spot sit empty for a few days. It may be that the bed was just overplanted in the first place. Give yourself some time to reevaluate it.

3. *Salvage.* Cut out all dead, weak, and intertwined branches on both plants. They may end up being lopsided, but they're still growing, and you can probably live with them.

4. *Transplant.* If you've got two healthy plants, it may be worth it to you to move one of them. Even a foot or two could make a big difference. Since this is the experimental side of gardening, it'll involve a bit of trial and error. You can increase a plant's chance of survival by watering it regularly, feeding it, and following the transplanting guidelines on pages 108–113.

Dying plants. Weeds are easily seen and disposed of, and if you have overgrown plants, you know they can be clipped back to look better, but a dying plant is trickier to recognize. And then, once you notice it, what do you do about it? You have a choice: replace it or nurse it along until it succumbs sometime later. Many experienced gardeners simply get rid of marginal plants before they become unsightly magnets for pests and disease. It's just one strategy towards keeping your yard healthy and looking lovely. Since all plants have a prescribed life span, a few plants will probably be on their way out at any given time, so you might as well toss them. A plant is usually dying if it has more than one of the following conditions: it's full of bare, graying, brittle branches; the foliage is distorted or discolored (yellowing, mottled, blackened, etc.); fewer than 40 percent of the branches are leafed out; or it no longer flowers.

Bare spots. While bare ground might not bother some gardeners, others don't like it. This problem has nothing to do with existing plants; it's just that you'd like to see your dirt covered with more plants.

Keep or Pitch—Exercise Your Authority

It's time for a little garden math. There may be some subtracting to do to get the bed ready before you can make your additions. Decide which plants you'll keep, which plants you'll move, and which ones you'll pitch (if any). While removing dead and dying plants seems logical, it may seem crazy to remove healthy shrubs and trees. Perennials, groundcovers, vines, grasses, and roses are relatively easy to subtract from your garden. Larger, more substantial landscape plants are problematic.

One of the hardest things to do is take out healthy plants, especially a tree, but you might have a compelling reason. Just because something has been in the same spot for 50 years doesn't mean it was well sited in the first place. You may just happen to be the gardener who must decide if that tree has finally outgrown its spot. It could have been the wrong tree in the wrong place. What was once a small, innocent sapling can turn into a limb-dropping, berry-laden, bug-infested weed tree that's dominating your lot, dictating every decision you make regarding your garden. You may want to take trees out if they obstruct views you want to reclaim; invade sewer and water lines; become a blow-over threat; outgrow the spot they're in and are too large to transplant; are so overpruned that they'll never recover an attractive shape; or are a nuisance because the leaf, branch, berry, or nut litter requires a lot of grooming time and leaves behind a mess on lawn or sidewalks.

If you're not sure you want to get rid of a tree, wait until fall (or the beginning of your dormant season) to make your decision. Spend spring and summer noting how much time it demands and how much pleasure it gives in return. Do the benefits outweigh the problems? Try to visualize your yard without it. Once you've taken it out, leave the spot bare for awhile. You may end up not replacing it. But if you do replace it, plant your more appropriate tree in the fall so it can settle in before the next growing season.

Since you're the garden manager, you have the ultimate say of what will be a member of your plant community. Exercise your authority; that's part of tailoring.

What Kind of Gardener Are You? Putting Your Personal Filter Together

The focus now turns from the flower bed to you. Your personal filter is really twofold. First you must connect with your Inner Gardener to find out why some gardening chores seem to never get done. After that, you'll discover the ways your Inner Gardener affects your behavior and approach to gardening—your Gardening Style.

Tune In to Your Inner Gardener

Your Inner Gardener is the part of you that knows how you honestly feel about gardening chores. Sometimes we listen to that little voice and sometimes we let our bigger dreams and desires run roughshod over our Inner Gardener. But honoring these feelings will help you achieve your personally tailored garden. When you're in tune with your Inner Gardener, you end up with a garden that is manageable for you.

Garden chores fall into one of five broad categories—cutting (pruning), weeding, hauling, watering, and digging. How you feel about doing any of these isn't a matter of right or wrong, it's simply your feelings about the actual work of gardening. You don't have to change your feelings, just acknowledge them.

To start, ask yourself what chores you resist and which you dutifully perform, or even enjoy. For some gardeners a good weeding session brings an immediate sense of satisfaction. Maybe that sounds dreadful to you, but you don't mind snipping at your laurel hedge every few months. If your goal is to spend minimal time in your yard, you shouldn't have a lot of difficult plants. So roses may not belong in your garden—unless you make an exception and decide you'll pamper them because they're worth it to you. At least you've consulted your Inner Gardener rather than ignoring it. If you don't listen to your Inner Gardener, it's easy to indulge in flights of garden fancy, but you can go only so long in that mode before either you or the garden falls apart.

To find your Inner Gardener, ask yourself :
- Am I happy gardening, and is it a satisfying hobby, or would I rather do anything else *but* garden?
- Am I afraid I'll make a mistake?
- Am I frustrated that I can't seem to achieve the garden I really want?
- Do I believe there are brown thumbs and green thumbs, and I am in the first group?
- Am I eager to garden when the weather is beautiful?
- Am I relieved when it rains on the weekend because I've got an excuse to get out of yard work?
- What amount of time "feels" right for me to spend in my yard?
- Do I wish I could have a nice-looking yard without doing anything to it?
- If I had enough money, would I hire out all of the garden chores?

Once you've evaluated your feelings about garden chores, it will make a huge difference in getting your garden to work well for you. If your Inner Gardener does not really like most garden work, you are going to have a hard time achieving anything but the simplest garden plan. However, if only specific chores are resisted, following are some suggestions for getting around them.

While you're shopping, consider the attributes of plants that fit with your likes and dislikes in gardening chores. If you're shopping without a list of specific plants, you'll find some of the information you need on plant tags; otherwise, you'll have to ask.

If you hate pruning

Look for:
- Slow growing plants—only minimal maintenance pruning will be necessary
- Words in plant descriptions noting plant form or branching pattern: compact, uniform, strong horizontal branching pattern, dwarf. If you see the words *nana, nanum, compacta, horizontalis* in the second half of the botanical name, it's a slow grower.
- Coniferous shrubs
- Sub-shrubs (mini-sized)

Be wary of:
- Hybrid tea roses. These persnickety roses require lots of specific pruning know-how.
- Fountain-like shrubs such as forsythia, mock orange, escallonia, spirea, or anything that comes with a recommendation to prune one third of the growth each year
- Hedges. Build a fence instead and be done with it!
- Vines that need seasonal cutting at just the right time (such as clematis, wisteria)
- Trying to cram a plant in a place that doesn't have enough room for its mature size. You will either be pruning to keep it in bounds, or letting it overshadow everything in the immediate vicinity.
- Anything that says it's a vigorous grower

If you hate picking off spent blossoms (deadheading)

Look for:
- Annuals that are easy to deadhead (picking off spent blooms) because the large flowers are on sturdy, erect stems (geraniums and gerbera daisies, for example), or annuals that can be sheared all at once (such as alyssum)
- Self-cleaning annuals, perennials, vines, and groundcovers (such as impatiens, blue flax). The flowers on these plants fall off when they are done blooming. Most, but not all, trees and shrubs are self-cleaning.

Be wary of:
- Annuals that must be deadheaded so they continue flowering (such as petunias, African daisies, marguerite daisies)
- Perennials that must be deadheaded so they continue flowering (such as coreopsis, black-eyed Susans).
- Shrubs that leave behind remnant flowers (lilacs and rhododendrons are examples). It doesn't hurt the plant if you don't take them off, but they'll look better, put out new growth faster, and remain more compact.
- Some spring blooming plants. You could be looking at dead flowers or seed pods all summer if you don't get around to tending them.

If you hate weeding

Look for:
- Groundcovers
- Mulch materials

- Creative ways to incorporate patios, paths, decks, etc., into your yard

Be wary of:
- Any plant with descriptions such as reseeds freely, fast spreading, free blooming, naturalizes freely, free flowering, vigorous, prolific, or fertile self-sowers (such as daisies). You'll be weeding frequently to keep them in check.
- Cramming together groundcovers that spread with aboveground runners (similar to strawberries)—unless you have lots of space to fill
- Perennials that reproduce and spread via underground runners (such as yarrow)
- Vines that root when they touch the ground and become groundcovers (such as ivy, vinca)
- Some native plants. Because these plants are well adapted to your region, they've developed means to ensure the continuation of the species—in other words, they reproduce willy-nilly.

If you hate watering

Look for:
- Drought-tolerant and native species that are adapted to your climate
- Succulents and sedums—these have water storing capabilities in their fleshy leaves and stems (such as hens and chicks)

Be wary of:
- Putting plants anywhere their natural water needs will not be met (for instance, if you put a bog plant in a dry place, you'll end up watering it frequently)

- Not grouping together plants with the same needs. If you must group dissimilar plants, look into irrigation as a possible solution.
- Putting annuals in pots—especially square pots, as the corners dry out

If you hate digging things up

Look for:
- Slow-growing varieties
- Plants that fit the space you want to fill

Be wary of:
- Perennials—if you don't like digging things up and moving them around, they may not be for you. Perennials described as having a spreading habit or being fast spreading grow from the center outward and will eventually require dividing if you want to keep the center "mother" plant from dying.
- Bamboo

YOUR INNER GARDENER INFLUENCES YOUR GARDENING STYLE

Your Gardening Style is the second half of your personal filter. It deals with your behavior, not your feelings, although your feelings directly influence it. Your style, in turn, influences how you approach gardening in general, the way you shop for plants, and what happens to those plants once they are put into your yard. As you better understand what's happening in your yard, you may realize you're more of a gardener than you originally thought—or that you want to be less of one. Once you get a handle on your current behavior in and around the garden, you'll see how it has played out in the choices you've made up to this point and whether or not your style has been over-shadowing your Inner Gardener.

To determine your gardening style, ask yourself:
- How much time do I actually spend gardening?
- Am I waiting until I have more time to tackle gardening?
- Have parts of my yard gotten away from me?
- Have I ever assumed that Mother Nature was tending my garden?
- What are the chores I continually put off and neglect, and which do I find satisfying?
- If I could hire out any one chore, what would it be?
- Do I know how to care for the plants I already have?
- Do I like to move things around in the yard?
- What tools do I own and actually use?

It is possible that your gardening style has evolved as the circumstances of your life have changed. It's not uncommon to experience an ebb and flow of interest in your garden over the years. Don't worry about trying to fit yourself into any one category; your personal approach might be a blend of the following gardening styles.

Gardening Style: The Impulsive Gardener

Impulsive Gardeners just dive in and try everything. After all, how hard can it be? They tend to plunk plants in the ground, expecting the plants to cooperate because that's what they *should* do. Plants grow, right? Enthusiastic and in love with the idea of gardening, they enjoy the process and are willing to spend the necessary time outside. Because

they love the whole gardening experience, they'll even worry and fuss over the plants that aren't doing so well.

Confirmed practitioners of plant tag gardening (see pages 56–58) and immediate results-oriented people, some Impulsive Gardeners feel sitting and reading about gardening just slows things down. Although Impulsive Gardeners have retained bits of gardening lore, usually there are gaps in their gardening knowledge, and this can get them into trouble when plant shopping. It doesn't take much to be seduced by a gorgeous flower or to scoop up gallons of plants they've overheard someone wax poetic over. They end up buying things for the wrong reasons, and plants can get stuffed anywhere in the garden, sometimes not in the best spot. Or worse, plants never manage to get into the ground at all.

For the Impulsive Gardener, any feeling of pitifulness comes from a lack of knowledge, not an unwillingness on the part of the Inner Gardener. They truly don't mind any of the chores that come with a particular plant; they just might not know what those chores are. Here the path to garden mastery is found by bridging the knowledge gap, either through obtaining one (or two) good garden book or developing a knowledgeable source.

Tips for Impulsive Gardeners

Tip Be clear about the reason for buying any plant. Does it fit in with the criteria you've established?

Tip Save impulse buying for annuals—group them into pots if you buy too many. After all, you can always buy another pot and potting soil.

Tip If plants aren't doing well, don't feel sorry for them. Resist any feeling of "I've spent money and effort on that" and expect ailing plants to recover. The health of your entire plant community depends upon you weeding out weak members.

Tip Learn how to transplant because you'll probably be doing it for awhile as you adjust your garden to match your ideals.

Gardening Style: The Harried Gardener

If only they had enough time! Some Harried Gardeners think they might actually like the whole gardening experience if they could just make the time. Gardening chores have to be accomplished in small increments, and their garden rarely matches their idea of how it should look because there is never enough time to do the maintenance work required, let alone any seasonal planting. Although Harried Gardeners don't have enough time to tackle the level of complexity they may want, many do envision becoming "real gardeners" sometime in the future.

For the Harried Gardener, feelings of pitifulness arise from time-related issues and may or may not be affected by lack of knowledge or the needs of their Inner Gardener. In fact, they may not even be aware of their Inner Gardener because they haven't had the luxury of gardening enough to know it well. The most important task for them is to match the time they have available to the time it takes to achieve their desired results. This could mean their garden plans need to be pared back until their circumstances change.

Tips for Harried Gardeners

Tip   Decide whether to hire out the chores you don't like to do, or replant to minimize them.

Tip   Let go of personal favorites if they're not doing well, until you can make time to accommodate them. You can always replant them later when you have more time.

Tip   Maintain a small variety of plants. Go for simplicity.

Tip   Pare your garden down to slow-growing, low-maintenance plants.

Tip   Continue with the same kinds of plants that are successful in your garden right now. You probably already know their names and needs. For variety try a different flower or leaf color, plant height, or blooming period. (For instance, you could end up with an assortment of rhododendrons that bloom from March through June.)

Tip   When adding plants, choose from the same broad

plant family as the varieties you already have in place. They'll have similar needs and soil requirements, so they won't need special treatment. This will take a certain amount of education, either from a book or by asking at the nursery. Those rhododendrons could be side-by-side with blueberries, andromeda, heather, Oregon grape, strawberry tree—all members of the diverse Ericaceae family.

Tip Rely on a few good flowering shrubs and trees for focal point color.

Tip Refrain from trimming shrubs into topiary or boxy forms. They usurp time because they'll require frequent attention. Let them assume their natural shapes.

Tip To reduce time spent shopping and experimenting, get a list of reliable, low-maintenance plants appropriate for your region from a local nursery or the county extension agent listed in your phone book.

Tip To gauge the amount of time a plant may require of you, you'll have to ask a knowledgeable person. Garden books are not set up to give that kind of specific information. For instance, they may mention that you have to deadhead, but not tell you how frequently.

Gardening Style: The Just-Tell-Me-What-to-Do Gardener

Because many people fall into this category, there are several variations of this gardener, but the common denominator is a lack of Inner Gardener awareness.

The Less-I-Know-the-Better Gardener. Some people feel their garden should be a onetime investment. After it's in place, they don't find a lot of pleasure in the continual maintenance process. They don't want or need superfluous information, just enough to care for the plants they have. Even better, they would like a professionally designed plan, or at least a good gardening source who can tell them what to buy, where to put it, and what to do for it. They view the trial-and-error method as a waste of time and energy.

The Timid Gardener. Timid Gardeners don't know where to start. They think they'd enjoy *doing* some gardening, but the overall process is bewildering and overwhelming. They're concerned they don't know enough and are afraid of doing something wrong. It seems everyone else is a better gardener.

The Reluctant Gardener. Gardeners falling into this category garden more out of guilt than desire. Maybe they'll get around to doing things they're "supposed" to do, or then again, maybe they won't. Chores have a way of getting put off, but because they like having a nice-looking yard, they eventually talk themselves into the work. It's just not how they'd choose to spend time.

The Disappointed Gardener. Gardeners in this category have experienced disappointment due to the gap between their optimistic expectations and the reality of their gardens. Each gardening season begins with high interest, but when things don't turn out as planned, they lose heart. It seems to them that "good" gardeners are born with green thumbs.

The key to success for Just-Tell-Me-What-to-Do Gardeners is to discover and stay in touch with their Inner Gardener. It should be the boss, ruling over every garden-related decision. When selecting plants, the first criteria filter used needs to be a personal one: Will this plant require more work or knowledge than I am willing to invest? Because most Just-Tell-Me-What-to-Do Gardeners probably rely on others to direct their plant choices, they need to be very, very specific in their questions and criteria. Their Inner Gardener may abhor a task that their "consultant" doesn't even consider a chore.

Tips for Just-Tell-Me-What-To-Do Gardeners

Tip Don't buy unfamiliar plants without informative plant tags. Ask for the information.

Tip Avoid demanding plants. Look for these low-maintenance plant attributes:
- Slow growing—less pruning expertise is required and they won't need attention for some time.

- Disease and pest resistance—less pest expertise required. Very little time will be spent trying to remedy bad situations with chemicals or natural methods. You won't need anyone to tell you what to do.
- Drought tolerance.
- Gardenworthy native plants.
- "Freeway plants"—the plants selected for interchanges and parking lot strips. They can survive with marginal care, as these sites typically receive minimal attention. Often overlooked by home gardeners, yet noted for their toughness, freeway plants are worth a second look.

Tip Ask for a list of reliable, low-maintenance plants at your favorite nursery or your county extension office instead of searching for them yourself.

Tip Add new plants slowly over time. Build on your successes. Be sure to check out the planting and transplanting tips on pages 108–113 to give them a fair start. When you feel confident your new plant is going to make it, add another.

Tip Avoid plants that need over-winter care to survive. One approach is to simply leave them alone. If they reappear in the spring, you managed to put the right plant in the right place. If they don't make it, consider them as annuals and decide if you want to replant each year.

Tip For instant gratification, buy annuals in gallon pots (at a minimum, look for pony packs) rather than starting plants from seed. Look for flower buds rather than open blooms. Your color show will last longer, and you'll be installing the plant before it hits its zenith.

Tip Reduce lawn and garden spaces by installing hardscapes—patios, ponds, and gazebos.

Tip If it's affordable, hire a designer to draw up a plan for your garden, or pay for a onetime consultation. Consider hiring a gardener to get your yard in shape at the beginning of the season. Have him or her tell you what to do to maintain it. Hire out the once-a-year chores.

What Kind of Garden Do You Want? Compiling Your Plant Filter

You've analyzed your site and figured out what kind of gardener you are, but have you ever thought about what it takes to get that picture-perfect garden? After reading through the plant groups and the accompanying reality checks, you may end up with a very different idea about what you want your garden to look like. Make sure the garden you're envisioning is right for you. Your plant filter is the last stop before the sifting process of Garden Tailoring begins.

Why you might not want a picture-perfect garden after all

It can be tough to narrow the gap between the fantasy of your dream garden and the reality of what's feasible, given your personal preferences about gardening. The promise implied on the front of seed packages and attractive garden magazine covers is very enticing. Who wouldn't want such sumptuous flowers and gardens? Picture-perfect magazine gardens don't look that way year round though. Those carefully arranged photos capture them at an optimal moment. They may be very nondescript or unattractive at other times of the year and end up requiring an unexpected amount of attention. Magazine gardens can be misleading when you're trying to recreate certain aspects of them, especially because those gardens may not even be from your region.

It may not be realistic for you to attempt duplicating a professional gardener's garden either. That wonderful garden is probably their passion and *raison d'être*. With careful planning and constant vigilance, your garden *could* achieve a period of sheer perfection. If you're determined to garden at that level, be prepared to conscientiously increase your knowledge and the time you devote to it. If you don't want to perform the work required and can't hire it out, then that fact should be reflected in your garden choices.

You can also be caught up in fantasy expectations if your heart is set on having certain plants that just won't survive in your garden conditions. Developing realistic plans should become easier as you progress through this book and the pieces fall into place.

Flowers equal work

When making choices that suit your level of gardening interest, a very broad rule of thumb (or at least one way to think about things) is that the further you move away from having a "green" yard composed only of trees, shrubs, ground covers, and foliage plants towards a colorful one, the more chores you'll have. This knowledge might keep you from buying every plant just for its flowers and consider some plants for their foliage instead.

In almost every case, it's fair to say that flowers equal work. Plants selected for colorful flowers typically come from the bulb, annual, perennial, rose, and vine categories. Depending on the types of plants and the number you have, expect to deadhead (cut off spent blooms), fertilize, divide, thin, replant, replace, install, trim, move around, stake, shop, plant seasonally, and increase your watering. Whew! You can control the amount of work by limiting the quantity and varieties, but those plants you want to flower throughout the growing season will require the most consistent attention of all.

In a yard filled with trees, shrubs, and groundcovers,

pruning will be the only major chore, and some of these plants may never even need pruning. But you don't have to have a garden composed only of trees and evergreen shrubs. Many flowering shrubs put on a colorful show and don't require deadheading or extra attention. It takes a bit more knowledge to ferret them out, but they can provide you with a punch of color without all the upkeep.

GETTING GARDEN SMARTS

On your journey to creating your garden, you'll find that the narrower your personal criteria, the more knowledge you need. That doesn't mean you must become an expert, though, because you can rely on several readily available resources to help you choose plants appropriately. If you enjoy strolling through garden aisles reading plant tags, you can glean enough information to use plant tag gardening. For increasingly complex organization, you need to know a bit more. Getting this additional information can be as sociable as asking around the neighborhood and at nurseries or as solitary as thumbing through a good gardening book.

Plant Tag Gardening

Reading plant tags is the most prevalent way of gathering information, although it might not be the most reliable. Tags are easily moved around or lost. Some consist simply of plant names and bar codes. And if you rely solely on tags, beware—you're gardening with only half-knowledge. There is actually a lot missing from tags. With only the small amount of space available on a tag to print instructions, you might get the impression that there isn't a lot to consider. But it can be quite frustrating when you unintentionally kill a plant because you didn't know what its entire cultural requirements were.

You can usually glean the following from plant tags:
- Name—common and botanical—and minimum planting instructions

- Mature size—at least the height, but not usually the depth and width
- Flower color (if notable) and bloom period
- Cultural requirements, or the "what is" of plant needs. You'll get a general sense (but not always the complete picture) of where to locate the plant and how much light it requires. If you're lucky, you might get the rest of the cultural requirements needed to help a particular plant thrive and flower: watering, quality of soil, and air temperature requirements.

The not-so-minor details omitted from plant tags

Some nurseries provide supplemental information on a sign above a group of plants rather than on individual tags. It's helpful to jot this stuff down so you don't have to remember it all. Or find out if the nursery has a handout, as some also provide this service.

Missing information usually includes:
- Pruning—when and how
- Fertilizing—what kind provides the most benefit
- Transplanting—whether or not a plant can tolerate being moved around
- Winterizing—how to care for it through the winter
- Any special tips particular to this plant
- Pests and diseases that love it

The limits of plant tag gardening

Even though plant tags provide just the basics, these basics can be translated into four reliable, simple methods of organization. If you choose to use plant tags exclusively, begin with your garden's needs first, honor your gardening style next, and *then* consult plant tags.

- **Cultural requirements**. Meeting a plant's cultural requirements is a given. You can't be successful at gardening and ignore this basic tenet, but arranging plants by similar watering, sunlight, and temperature needs can be another guiding principle.

- **Height**. Plants are easily arranged by putting the tall plants in the back of the bed and stair-stepping the others down to the edge. You can also have an island of plants, with tall ones in the middle and the rest arranged by diminishing height in concentric circles.
- **Specific flower color**. Maybe you would like to have a blue garden or just add a blue flowering plant. This is easily achieved with plant tag gardening. Gardens don't have to be color-coordinated, because Mother Nature certainly doesn't bother. Using color as a criterion can be simple or become very complicated, depending upon the parameters you set.
- **Bloom time**. You can have a bed that continually has something in bloom. You'll have to plant it in staggered stages. Visiting nurseries and garden centers during the time you need a new flowering plant is a great way to accomplish this.

If you don't want to remember your plants' names, leave the tags on, or partially bury them near the plant. If you have any future problems you can get answers quickly, as you'll be able to start your questions with "My skimmia. . . ." instead of "I have this plant with green leaves and green bugs. . . ."

DEVELOP YOUR SOURCES—BUT BEWARE THE GARDEN EVANGELIST

If the information on a plant tag leaves something to be desired, and you don't use a garden book, you'll need to develop personal sources. While knowledgeable friends, neighbors, nursery employees, and your county extension agent can act as valuable founts of information, be wary of Garden Evangelists. These folks are devoted to gardening and assume you want to be involved at the same level. They can spend hours in their garden never noticing the time. They've never met a high-maintenance plant they didn't like or thought too difficult to grow. To get exactly the right plant from these zealots, you'll have to craft questions that get to the heart of your criteria, not theirs. By the time you've reached the end of Garden Tailoring, you'll know how to do this.

FIND ONE (OR TWO) GOOD GARDENING BOOKS

The Pitiful Gardener's Handbook is designed to be a helping hand steering you through the bare essentials of gardening. However, unlike other garden books, it focuses considerable attention on the kind of attitude adjustments that enable you to be more successful in spite of yourself. It shows you how to pick your way through staggering amounts of garden information and glean what's useful to you. But it isn't a complete guide to the "basics" and beyond. If you'd like to move farther along the gardening path, another book or two will enlighten your journey.

There are thousands of gardening books, written from every point of view imaginable. But not all garden books are created equally. They can be divided roughly into three categories of information—gardening basics, plant encyclopedias, and specialty books focused on a specific aspect of gardening or plants.

Basic gardening can be covered by anything from a slim volume to an all-encompassing reference manual. What you should expect from your one good gardening book is easy access to the information you need: maintenance how-to's, a plant compendium illustrated with photographs or drawings, and plant lists covering different site situations and design considerations. Because the topic of gardening is so huge, there are literally hundreds of ways to organize the information. Books that go in for more esoteric organization, such as taking a season and highlighting certain plants, might bury the things you want to know under mounds of other information.

The most useful plant encyclopedia (a book focused on plants exclusively) will have everything you wished was on plant tags, and more. Although the garden basics are usually glossed over, some encyclopedias include plant lists for different site considerations. If you have a book composed solely of plant lists, it will work better in conjunction with a plant encyclopedia.

The opposite of the all-encompassing reference books are specialty books focused on one topic, plant, or technique. If you really get hooked on a particular subject or want more in-depth instruction than your one good garden book provides, the specialty titles will satisfy you like nothing else can. You'll find a list of books covering all three categories of gardening information in Appendix A, page 155–157.

When you consult a garden book filled with pictures, you get a sense of the "whole enchilada." While plant tags might mention flower color, there won't be much about what the actual plant looks like. Catalogs and seed packages brim over with flashy photographs of flowers, but rarely show the entire plant. Sometimes you want to know exactly what you're getting.

Your garden book should give information in a straightforward manner. When you're shopping you often encounter garden lingo that begs for interpretation. Like real estate ads, you have to read between the lines on tags, seed packages, and catalogs. Sometimes a rangy plant possesses photogenic, gorgeous flowers, but they're attached to a five foot bush of the ugliest foliage you've ever seen. "Back of the border" probably means tall and rangy, with unattractive foliage. Get out the stakes and twine if you find the word "nodding" describing a plant you want. You'd better really like a plant that "self sows freely" because your yard could be filled with its progeny (weeds) the next year. "Vigorous" might crowd out every other plant in the vicinity. Your one good gardening book should tell it like it is.

KNOWLEDGE CREATES OPTIONS

Your gardening book will also give you the means to embellish your criteria to plan a more focused garden. Complexity requires contemplation—in other words, it takes some thought and research to pull it together. You can find what you need for these mental exercises right at your fingertips. A good gardening book will let you choose plants with exactly the qualities you want.

- **Foliage color, size, and shape**. A garden-worthy plant is much more than a pretty flower, although flowers are often the starting point for gardeners. When you choose plants because of their interesting leaf shapes, sizes, and colors, you add layers of sophistication to your garden without significantly increasing your workload.

- **Fragrance**. This can be as simple as selecting a scented rhododendron over an unscented one. However, flower color is frequently the driving force when plants are hybridized for the garden industry, and attributes such as fragrance are often sacrificed. That's why many hybridized tea roses are dazzling in color but lacking in scent.

- **Fall and winter interest**. Plants selected because they have interesting bark, berries, seed pods, and pleasing branching structure can become focal points at a time of year when most yards are rather blasé. The trick is to look at the whole plant and how it changes over the year, instead of focusing on only one aspect such as flowers. A garden containing an interesting array of features can be just as visually complex and stimulating as one filled with a bounty of flowers—and a lot less work to boot!

- **Wildlife attractors**. Trees and shrubs provide haven and food for wildlife. Plants attractive to birds and small animals have remnant seedpods and berries that hang on through the winter months, so they may also be of visual interest to you.

- **Edible landscapes**. Many fruit trees, vegetables, herbs, and berry plants also function as ornamental plants. County extension offices should be able to provide lists and ideas.

- **Plants to recreate an ecological niche**. It will take research to create a certain look such as a desert, woodland, or bog, because you have to go beyond finding plants with the same cultural requirements to finding ones that actually would be present in that particular setting.

- **Flower color timed to blooming periods**. This requires the most research and planning of all. Your garden becomes increasingly complex if you want to have a specific color last all season, some colorful plants year-round, or have your bed change color each season (i.e., yellow in spring, blue in summer, orange in fall). In addition to annuals, you will have to rely more on perennials and find specific flowering shrubs. You can visit nurseries during each season that you want blooming plants to see what's available at that specific time, and you'll probably also spend some time with a book of plant descriptions and lists.

THE PLANT CATEGORIES

It's been said before, but an important part of tailoring your garden is learning which plants you're willing to care for, because even though you may not like doing a particular chore, there's no getting around the fact that plants do require certain things. As you make your selections, it's helpful to know the characteristics of the broad plant categories they come from, so you can get a feel for what the plants will need from you over the long run. In each plant category you'll find a brief description; reasons to have many, a few, or totally exclude them from your collection; and tips for maintaining them.

For the first two growing seasons, it pays to be fairly attentive while any plant is establishing itself in your garden. After that, most plants become more independent. Although you must ensure that plants are well sited and receive enough water, you don't have to feed or groom them. When you do, you enhance the quality of your plant, but it will continue to live whether or not this is part of your routine.

Garden plants can be divided into nine general categories,

listed here in the order of the work involved to maintain them at minimal levels. Having arranged them in this order, it must also be noted that within each category are individual plants that defy the ranking—it seems as if there's always an exception to any rule! It's hard to predict if you'll ever experience certain problems within any plant category (except for hybrid tea roses, which are highly susceptible) because many contributing factors can influence whether particular plants will be troublesome or not. Hopefully, yours won't be!

In order, from lowest to highest maintenance, the categories are:

> groundcovers
> vines
> trees
> shrubs
> bulbs
> antique shrub roses
> annuals
> perennials
> hybrid tea roses

GROUNDCOVERS

Groundcovers are the next best thing to having someone else weed for you. They are low-growing and shallow-rooted plants that can spread rapidly. They make gardening easy. Consider them a helping-hand kind of plant, keeping your weed populations in check and filling in bare spaces. In addition, they're easy to grow, most requiring little care. Once you establish the right groundcover in the right place, you barely have anything else to do. Many reproduce freely and are easily transplanted from one area to another.

Reasons to have groundcovers:

- It's the only plant category that saves you more work than it causes.
- They help solve problem areas, preventing water run-off and soil erosion from slopes. Some are fire retardant; others serve as lawn replacements.
- There's a variety suitable for just about any kind of bare spot.
- They grow quickly and soon give the garden a mature look.
- Thinning is simple—just pull out whole plants.
- It's easy to see weeds because you know whatever is coming up through the groundcover doesn't belong.

Reasons not to have ground covers:

- Vigorous groundcovers may become a nuisance, choking out and running over other plants if they're not given enough room.

Tips for growing groundcovers

Tip Fertilize areas densely planted with groundcovers. Because all plants are in competition for a limited amount of available nutrients, fertilizing ensures each one receives enough food. If you don't, your plants can remain small and become puny.

Tip Don't use groundcovers under mildew-prone plants such as deciduous azaleas and roses, especially if the groundcover is over six inches tall. Taller groundcovers interfere with air circulation, promoting mildew.

Tip Some groundcovers will benefit from deadheading or shearing and may bloom again. If you don't trim, they end up looking a bit shaggy. Shearing rejuvenates groundcovers such as thyme and alyssum; deadheading tidies up groundcovers such as ajuga and thrift.

Tip Mulch around slow-growing groundcovers. When you don't, weeds get a toehold while you're waiting for the groundcover to fill in. The weeds manage to undo one of the main advantages of planting groundcovers in the first place.

Tip Keep an eye on fast-growing groundcovers and thin them if necessary. You'll know they need to be thinned when they begin to choke out their neighbors.

VINES

Vines and climbers quickly add maturity to your garden with a simple investment of yearly maintenance. It takes very little effort to be successful with vines. Many have showy flowers or foliage that require no deadheading or cleanup from you. Give them a good place to roost and they'll take off. They do need plenty of room to roam, twine, and climb. Without support, vines act as groundcovers, snaking through the garden in search of a place to climb.

Reasons to have vines:
- Many have beautiful flowers.
- They go where other plants don't, climbing over areas of substandard soil.
- They can cover a structure.
- They can visually fill in an area quickly.
- They can take a certain amount of neglect.
- The canes of some vines have the capability to reroot and create new plants every time they touch the ground, thus filling in bare spots.

Reasons not to have vines:

- Since some vines will reroot every so often, creating new plants, they'll have to be pulled out of areas where they're not wanted.
- Ivies go wherever they want to, since they have aerial roots. They can crack bricks, dislodge shingles, and strangle trees.
- Lots of dead branches under new growth weighs the plant down. It can become very heavy, flattening support structures.
- Your garden lacks an adequate place to grow or support one.
- You don't want to do the work to keep the vine under control.

Tips for Growing Vines

Tip   Give vines adequate structural support to scramble over. If the support is not adequate, a vine will eventually pull it down.

Tip   Read the plant tag to note its eventual mature size, then provide enough room to roam. You could be in for years of pruning a large plant to keep it tamed.

Tip   Thin a little every now and then. Every few years after a vine has reached maturity, prune as much of the dead wood beneath the plant mass as you dare. Without this kind of maintenance pruning, the supporting structure could crumble under the weight of the vine.

Tip If you let a climbing vine roam through a large tree, fertilize both. They will be competing for the same water, food, and sunlight. Without assistance from you, nothing tragic will occur, other than both plants will have less than ideal growth. *A word of caution:* Be wary of letting ivy scramble up a tree; it ends up taking over the host, and eventually kills it.

FOCUS ON CLEMATIS

While most varieties of vines aren't particular when, or even if, they're pruned, clematis have specific needs. Clematis are divided into three categories that cue you when to prune so that flower buds aren't accidentally snipped off.

- If your clematis blooms in the spring, lightly prune for shape within one month after it's done blooming. If the vine is going off in a direction you don't like, this is the time to deal with it. Spring-blooming clematis set buds for the next year fairly soon after flowering, so if you prune too late, you'll cut them off.

- Clematis that bloom in late spring and summer are pruned in either the fall or very early spring. Pinch off the large seeds pods after the bloom period.

- Mid-summer and fall bloomers are treated differently than spring bloomers. Rather than snipping back a few long tendrils, cut down the entire plant in either the late fall or early spring. For the first couple of years, take it down to a foot above ground level. After it matures, whack it back to two feet high each season.

TREES

Trees are dynamic members of your landscape, influencing the environment around them. More than any other purchase for your garden, trees make an impact on your lot. Even though a tree stays put, over time it will alter what's around it. What you may have bought as a decorative item ends up bringing continual, evolutionary change to the garden.

Trees affect how you end up gardening around them, shifting plants around to find ones that will grow beneath them. A tree also modifies the temperature in its vicinity, sheltering other plants from extreme weather. They add more liveliness to a garden than any other plant group since they provide habitat for many forms of wildlife. They may not look as if they're doing much, but trees are busy affecting everything around them.

Reasons to have trees:
- Trees add monetary value to your landscape.
- They add visual interest.
- They create habitat.
- After the first two years, the tree itself isn't much work except for pruning and raking leaves.
- Some trees have beautiful spring or early summer blossoms or fall leaf color.
- Because of the shade they eventually cast, you'll come to know a variety of shade-loving plants.

Reasons not to have trees:
- You have no interest in getting to know a variety of shade-loving plants.
- A tree can become a liability if it's planted in the wrong spot.

- They'll rob surrounding plants of nutrients.
- You don't want or need shade.
- The habitat they create brings in wildlife you don't want.
- You may not like specific trees because of what falls out of them.
- You don't like raking leaves.
- Evergreens have dense, dry shade all year long, severely limiting what can grow under them.
- It's causing you more work than you want.

Tips for growing Trees

Tip Use research and apply your personal filters to get exactly the right tree for the spot you are filling. Tree remedies are often costly. After all, you're not dealing with a few pansies. You could end up topping

---

FOCUS ON STREET TREES

When you have a suburban or urban yard, the selection of appropriate trees narrows. Desirable street trees are small, fit under wires and poles, have moderate watering needs, don't have invasive roots that destroy sidewalks, and don't drop lots of messy litter. To help, many cities and towns have developed a list of trees that are compatible in the high-traffic areas where people and cars mix. Some municipalities have even compiled lists of trees not allowed in public right-of-ways, so check with the public works or park departments. Your county extension agent may also have such a list.

---

the tree to preserve a view (fraught with its own bugaboos, see page 137); cutting it down to preserve sidewalks, driveways, water mains, roofs; or removing it because of unexpected leaf, berry, seed, or branch litter.

Tip   For the first two years after planting the tree, water it deeply every two weeks during dry periods. It generally takes a tree two to three years to establish itself, putting down strong roots and getting poised for active growth. Trees often go into shock after they're planted. Without care, they can become stunted, take a long time to recover, or even die.

SHRUBS

Shrubs are the dependable, unsung heroes of the garden, requiring very little care. They are some of the least demanding plants you'll ever maintain. Considered the "bones" of the garden, they lend visual structure to flower beds. They also provide a backdrop for flowering plants. Evergreen shrubs add interest during the winter when flowers have died back. In the spring, flowering shrubs deliver a burst of color in one place. Although spring is the main blooming period for most shrubs, plenty of shrubs bloom at other times of the year. However, these may not be as readily available and you'll have to ask for them.

Reasons to have shrubs:
- They're easy to care for, dependable, and unfussy.
- If you let the plant grow into its natural form, you only have light trimming and dead stuff to remove.
- Many are tolerant if you get off to a bad start and accidentally prune them badly.

- If you must deadhead, you'll only have to do it after they're done blooming.

Reasons not to have shrubs:
- They can take up a lot of room—you could have two to three perennials instead if color is important to you (this is really a design consideration).
- You can't extend the bloom period by deadheading. If you want a longer color season, you'll be better off choosing from annual, perennial, and rose categories.

Tips for growing shrubs

Tip Let the shrub mature into its natural form before attempting any shape pruning. If you begin pruning too soon, you may end up committed to a rigid regimen of pruning.

Tip Make sure the mature size of the shrub matches the place you're putting it in. If you don't, you set yourself up for any or all of the scenarios detailed in The Dead, The Dying, and The Ugly on pages 32–36.

BULBS

Bulbs magically pop up long after you've forgotten the work you've done. Corms, tubers, rhizomes, and tuberous roots are usually lumped together in the bulb category. Although they are different, they all function as tidy little nutrient storage units that contain everything the plant needs to grow the following year. The only missing ingredients are soil, warmth, and water.

Early spring bulbs add considerable cheer since they spring into action at a time of year when little or nothing else is blooming. The great thing about bulbs is that you can just plunk them in the ground, kick back, and wait for armloads of flowers to appear. Bulbs are an easy way to add vibrant color to your garden if you can tolerate the dying foliage while the bulbs convert sunlight into nutrients for the next year. Once installed, they only require a yearly maintenance of grooming and fertilizing.

Reasons to have them

- Bulbs give you a burst of color.
- They're fairly reliable—put them into the ground and they pop up on their own.
- It's possible to stagger the planting of summer bulbs such as gladiolas every two weeks and create an extended bloom time in your yard.
- Bulbs have an internal clock and will bloom "on time" even if you get them into the ground later than you planned.

Reasons not to have them

- Some multiply themselves and eventually need to be dug up and divided.
- Some diminish and produce less over the years.
- The flowers last a short time compared to the length of time the foliage is left behind.
- You forget where you planted them and accidentally dig them up or plant over the top of them.

Tips for growing bulbs

Tip Let foliage die naturally, rather than cutting it off as soon as the flowers fade. Without leaves, sunlight cannot be converted into plant nutrients for the following year's flowers. Flower output will diminish each passing year.

Tip If you don't like dying foliage, treat bulbs as annuals. Toss out the old bulbs after they're done blooming, and replant new ones at the appropriate time of year. The only downside to doing this is the added expense and effort.

Tip Another way to handle dying foliage is to put other kinds of bulbs or plants in the bed to disguise the wilting leaves. The only consequence is that the bed may become overcrowded. If the plants begin to look stunted, you may need to give supplemental food and water.

Tip Find out if the bulbs, corms, tubers, rhizomes, and tuberous roots you are considering need to be divided on a regular basis. If they are not divided, they'll become congested and less vigorous, producing poorer flowers as years go by.

THE OTHER "BULBS"—NOT AS STRANGE AS THEY SOUND

Although the words corm, rhizome, tuber, and tuberous roots may not be a part of your vocabulary, their flowers are quite familiar.

Corms—Gladiolas, crocus, freesia, crocosmia, ixia.

Rhizomes—Iris, calla lily.

Tubers—Begonias, potatoes.

Tuberous Roots—Dahlia, cyclamen, ranunculus, some peonies, sweet potatoes.

True Bulbs—Tulips, onions, daffodils, lilies, grape hyacinth, hyacinth, fritillaria.

Tip   Plant bulbs in groups of three or more. They help hold each other up and lessen the need for staking. In addition, groups of flowers make stronger color statements.

Tip   If you plan to keep your bulbs, feed them after they are done blooming. Fertilizer renews bulbs, prolonging their lives, and produces strong, healthy flower displays the following year.

ANTIQUE SHRUB ROSES

Antique shrub roses are the original rose. Considering how easy these roses are to maintain compared to their more popular, fussier cousins the tea roses, it's surprising that they aren't used more often in today's gardens. These were the popular roses in your great-grandma's day. Being a shrub, they're more carefree and hardy. In fact, shrub roses are so hardy that the tender branches of tea roses are grafted onto their roots.

You have to search for antique shrub roses, sometimes through specialty nurseries and catalogs. It's not that they're rare, they're just not in demand. Look for them under the moniker of antique roses, rugosas, moss roses, hybrid perpetuals, cabbage roses, polyanthas, gallicas, albas, or dog roses.

Antique shrub roses look more like an actual shrub, growing large and bushy. Most are extremely fragrant, but since they come in limited colors and may only bloom once a year, as other shrubs do, they're often passed over for the flowers of tea roses. Still, antique shrub roses are definitely worth consideration if you want an undemanding flowering plant.

Reasons to have antique shrub roses:

- They are easy to care for.
- They have no special watering needs.
- They don't need enriched soil.
- They're disease resistant compared to the susceptible hybrid teas.
- Many are fragrant—they're known as perfume roses.
- You don't have to have specialized pruning knowledge like you do for hybrid teas.

Reasons not to have antique shrub roses:

- They need a lot of sun.
- They need a lot of room—they're much bigger than hybrid teas.
- They don't have quite the color range of hybrid teas.
- Most have either spring or summer blooms, not continuous spring to fall blooms such as hybrid teas.
- Deadheading won't prolong the blooming period for the majority of shrub roses.
- Although they are becoming more popular, they are still difficult to find.

Tips for growing antique shrub roses

Tip If your antique shrub rose spreads by underground runners, and begins making unwanted appearances in other parts of your garden, be sure to dig those runners out.

Tip Transplant in the spring. Prune it back and then dig it up. Transplanting when it's dormant won't disrupt the growing cycle, and cutting it back first makes it easier to handle.

ANNUALS

Annuals provide instant color gratification. Decorating the garden with annuals is akin to putting up a Christmas tree—you've got colorful decorations up for the season in a relatively short amount of time. Because their mission is to produce enough seed to replicate themselves for the next year, these little powerhouses will bloom like crazy with only a bit of help. In one growing season they sprout, flower, go to seed, and die. The mainstays of pots, annuals aren't difficult to care for, they're just time consuming. A good way to remember the difference between annuals and perennials is that you plant annuals annually and perennials are always, perennially, with you.

Reasons to have annuals:
- Annuals are frequently on sale.
- They're common and easy to find.
- They're easy to put in and take out.
- You can try different things each year; it's no big deal if you botch it up.
- You get instant color without the wait.
- They have longer bloom periods than most perennials.
- They're primed to flower when you buy them.
- Shopping can be really easy if you plant the same thing each year.
- Annuals are great for pots.

Reasons not to have annuals:
- If you rely on them as your main source for color to cover big areas, the cost of replanting adds up over the years.
- You have to put them in and take them out each year.
- They need continuous watering in the summer;

annuals in pots require more watering than any other plant group.

- Most have to be deadheaded all season long.
- Removing all the plants from the flower bed at the end of the season is a chore you don't have with other plant categories.
- Most of the bed will be bare during the winter.
- Some are susceptible to pests that enjoy munching on tender blossoms and stalks.

Tips for growing Annuals

Tip More so than with other plants, annuals benefit from deadheading and feeding. Your annual will reward you by producing more flowers for a longer period of time. Annuals do their thing for one season. Depending on the species, without your helping hands the flowering period might last only a few weeks.

Tip Use potting soil for annuals in pots, not garden soil. Potting soil drains better, is lighter for root growth, and doesn't harbor pests or diseases. If you use potting soil, you'll also need to fertilize, since there are no nutrients in sterilized soil (see Potting Soil, page 125). If you decide to use garden soil, be extra vigilant for soil-borne pests and diseases.

Tip Water annuals in pots regularly. Pots dry out quickly, and uneven watering habits weaken plants.

Tip Group annuals together in your flower beds, or congregate the pots to simplify watering and fertilizing chores. You could find yourself forced into dragging the hose all over your yard and, worse, not watering adequately during a dry spell.

PERENNIALS

Perennials are the athletes of the garden. They are flowering plants that are permanent members of the garden, coming back on their own each year. However, some of them may not return to quite the same place. They are on the move via various modes such as runners, reseeding, or plantlets splitting off from the mother plant. They spread, wander, jump, and pop up in new places, so your garden design won't stay the same without intervention. Your garden design may also be more complicated because perennials don't grow at the same time and rate, and some will become overshadowed by others. Still, the bountiful choice of color is the reason flower lovers have them; a number of famous artists had beautiful perennial gardens because playing with color is fun.

In the beginning, perennials are easy; the real work comes later as you try to maintain your garden design. If you're content to just let them follow their own inclinations and allow the garden to shift and change, then you have less to do. To keep perennials in shape, gardeners divide and split the plants apart. There's no hard and fast rule about how often perennials should be divided—it depends on what you have.

Reasons to have perennials:
- You can have color for a long period by staggering plant types.
- You don't have to replant each year.
- There's a bigger selection of plant types and sizes than annuals.
- It's possible to group plants together by color and bloom time.
- They're easy to move around.

- They help control soil erosion on slopes and in rockeries.
- Since many perennials multiply easily, you can have plenty of new plants.

Reasons not to have perennials:
- You have to deadhead some varieties during the season to keep them flowering.
- At the end of the season you have to clean up the bed, cutting back dead stalks and spent leaves, or else suffer the raggedy remains.
- Since you can't expect most varieties to flower all season like annuals, you'll need to have several different kinds of perennials to accomplish the same effect.
- Getting perennials to stay where you want can be difficult.
- Plants left unattended can look overgrown and messy.
- You can have a hole ringed by plantlets if you're not inclined to divide a spreading perennial that has died out in the center.
- They may attract pests that feed on the tender shoots emerging from the ground.

Tips for growing perennials

Tip Divide or pull off the offspring that congregate around the edges of the mother plants. Offspring usurp all the nutrients, cause the center to wane, and leave a ring of new growth around a dead plant.

Tip Find out how any perennial you are considering reproduces. You may not be up to the challenge of dealing with its many future offspring.

Tip Resist overplanting new perennials, giving them enough space for their mature size. You could witness a population explosion. The multitudes will elbow each other out for the limited amount of nutrients and sunshine, and they'll be plagued by mildew from overcrowding.

HYBRID TEA ROSES

Hybrid tea roses are the queen of the garden and command your attention. Hybrid tea, floribunda, and grandiflora roses are the most popular of the flowering shrubs. They're one of the few that flower all season long, and they come in the widest variety of colors. But these roses don't occur naturally. They are an entirely manmade phenomenon, part of a contrived, sped-up evolutionary process. They are rather like poodles in that respect—a long way from their original source. In the rose world, it's a relentless

drive towards the newest creation. The hybrids that have emerged from this process are frost sensitive, and so they've been grafted onto shrub rose rootstock. If you want a lot of color in a small space and you want roses, then go for hybrid teas. Just know that tea roses require the most work of any plant group.

Reasons to have hybrid tea roses:
- Roses have beautiful flowers from spring to fall, outlasting most other flowering plants.
- You can get nearly any color you want.
- Many are fragrant.

Reasons not to have hybrid tea roses:
- Roses alter your behavior more than any other plant.
- They can be extremely time consuming as they're continually hungry and thirsty.
- They require full sun six hours a day, and your yard is too shady.
- They require deep watering at least twice a week during dry spells.
- They're susceptible to bugs and blight, needing constant vigilance.
- You must protect the graft during severe winter conditions.
- Roses like to be groomed continually throughout their growing season.

Tips for Growing Hybrid Tea Roses

Tip Maintain good air circulation between plants. Don't congregate them close to each other or other plants; leave at least three feet between them. (Check the tag or your references to determine how large the bush will grow.) Reduced air circulation means increased chance of disease. It also means pests and diseases have an easy time jumping from one bush to another.

Tip Water at the ground level. Avoid using overhead sprinklers. Greedy roses need regular deep watering, not light sprinkles. Keep your water source close to the ground to lessen the chance of mildew spreading on leaves, where it is a significant problem in some regions.

Tip Pick leaves off all stems up to eight inches from the ground. No dire consequences will result if you don't remove them; however, two diseases—rust and blackspot—can lie waiting on soil surfaces or fallen, tainted leaves. These diseases are easily spread via backsplash from falling rain and overhead sprinkling. Removing leaves from the lower eight inches gives them nowhere to go.

Tip Get rid of aphids ASAP. They'll suck the life out of tender parts of your plants. You can kill aphids with either chemicals or organic methods. Chemicals are most effective. Use rose fertilizers that include a poison to kill everything feeding on your rose. They're called "systemics," which means you're introducing something to the entire plant, not just spot treating. You may find yourself tied into a chemical regimen every six weeks. Organic managers can release ladybugs or try encouraging small birds such as chickadees to feed on the aphids. You can also squish aphids by hand or use soapy sprays.

Tip When planting the bush, place the graft slightly above ground level. When the graft is placed below ground level, the original plant your tea rose was grafted onto will be encouraged to sucker.

Tip Cut off canes (suckers) growing up from below the graft. If the rootstock sends up its own shoots and you don't remove them, they will overwhelm the grafted hybrid tea. It's still a rose, but it won't be the one you thought you bought. You can tell that the suckers are taking over when there are two distinct flowers on one bush.

Tip Don't forget to remove any mulching materials you put on the graft to protect it during the winter. When the weather warms and the graft is left buried under mulch, suckering and rot may result.

Tip Make a shallow little basin around your rose bush. Water doesn't have a chance to run off and goes directly to the roots instead.

Tip Transplant when dormant. If you don't, your rose may drop a copious amount of leaves, compromising overall plant health. If you do have to transplant while it's actively growing, water generously and feed soon after. (See the tips on planting and transplanting on pages 108–113 for additional help.)

Look Before You Leap

Now that you've begun to sort through gardening and thought about your relationship with it, it would be oh, so tempting, to run out and shop for plants. After all, you're going to do it right this time! But hold your horses—to truly get it right you need to have a game plan.

Microsolving—The Pitiful Approach

We are often tempted to select a plant because it was blooming in a favorite color, on sale, looked about the right size, or for some other momentary consideration. However, success can be rather dubious under such circumstances, for neither the plant's needs nor what it was placed next to were considered. This method of plant buying is called microsolving.

Step 1. Discover a bare spot in your flower bed.

Step 2. Go to the nursery.

Step 3. Buy an attractive plant.

Step 4. Stick it in the dirt.

Step 5. Leave it to the forces of nature.

Step 6. Rediscover the same bare spot sometime in the future.

Macrosolving—The Garden Tailoring Approach

Your garden is created by a variety of accumulated, individual choices. Macrosolving is a nearly foolproof technique to gratify your gardening needs. It helps you look at the big picture before buying plants. When you macrosolve you combine everything you've discovered about your Inner Gardener, your gardening style, the site conditions in your yard, the way you want your yard to look, and the plants you know you'll care for. Now, instead of just walking into a plant store knowing you want *something* to fill an empty space, you enter with a solid idea of what the best plant should do for you. Experienced gardeners do this intuitively; in time it can become second nature to you too.

Step 1.   Scrutinize the bare spot in your yard, noting its general physical aspects.

Step 2.   Go to the nursery and ask pertinent questions about appropriate plants for that spot or check a good gardening book.

Step 3.   Used your filters to determine the most suitable plant and buy it.

Step 4.   Put the right plant in the right place.

Step 5.   Nurture it for at least two growing seasons.

Step 6.   Check occasionally for plant health.

PUTTING FILTERS TO WORK FOR YOU

In step one, you're addressing the Site Filter. This is when the importance of sun patterns, soil conditions, how much room you're trying to fill, and any existing temperature quirks come into play. Although all gardeners start with this filter, the site filter is where Impulsive Gardeners run into the most trouble. When the mood strikes them to go garden shopping, the attractiveness of a plant can induce them to ignore existing yard conditions. Keeping the site uppermost in your thoughts when considering a plant will spare you a great deal of garden rework.

In step two, *before* you buy, use the Garden Smarts method you find the most appealing (a good gardening book, plant tag, or other source) to get accurate information about a plant's cultural requirements. If you rely on personal sources for plant information, beware of Garden Evangelists who can unwittingly talk you into plants requiring work you detest. Remember which chores you hate doing, and select from appropriate plant groups to avoid those tasks.

In step three, using both Plant and Personal Filters puts the focus specifically on you. Different gardeners can end up with different plants (albeit appropriate for them) for the same site. Crafting your criteria into a tangible, concrete list helps you to be articulate when hunting for plants.

Be aware that your choices of plants will narrow dramatically if you have a number of gardening chores you want to avoid. That's how personal filters impact the plant filter. But you will be in charge of both shopping choices and your garden! For example, Harried Gardeners know time is precious. Don't forget to take into consideration which chores you'll do and what kinds of things you don't have time for. If the "right" plant for your site is high-maintenance, it isn't the "right" plant for you.

Let your Inner Gardener lead the way. This is especially important for Just-Tell-Me-What-to-Do Gardeners. Although you may have to compromise criteria you hoped to get in your plant filter, satisfying your Inner Gardener (using your personal filter) will ultimately save you future disappointment and frustration.

When you reach step four, that "right plant" will

undoubtedly be yours once you read the tips coming up in **Shopping Savvy**. How to get it into the right place, the right way is laid out in The Immutable Laws of Planting and Transplanting page 108-113.

Then all that's left to do is take care of that plant as mentioned in steps five and six. Although the first two years are a critical period, a bit of continued extra care goes a long way. The third section of the book, Garden Management, will give you the details to do that well.

And there you have it—successful gardening in a nutshell.

❧ SHOPPING SAVVY ❧

Although you've been able to decide on the perfect plant or plants, where to buy them becomes another consideration. The following guidelines offer you some whys and wherefores about the places where you can show off your shopping savvy.

DOES IT MATTER WHERE I BUY PLANTS?

Yes and no. Each type of retail outlet has carved out a specific niche in the huge garden industry, giving you a variety of services and value.

GROCERY AND DISCOUNT STORES

What they do well:
- Frequent sales and end-of-season markdowns
- Plants that are usually the hardiest and most likely to succeed in your climate

Watch out for:
- Plants may be stressed from a long journey in the back of a dark truck, exposed to extreme temperatures, so care for your purchase right away.
- Note plant tags marked as perennials. In the region where they were originally propagated, they are perennials, but if you have a different climate, you may have to regard them as annuals.
- The stock is usually displayed at the entrance of the store or on blacktop parking lots, so it is alternately stressed from heat, car fumes, overexposure to the

sun, and under- or overwatering. They may wilt when you finally get them into the ground.

- Don't automatically buy that front-and-center pony pack. Look in the back of the shelves for the freshest stock because sometimes the older stock is "faced" to the front. Buy shade lovers from the bottom racks, sun lovers from the upper racks.

HOME IMPROVEMENT STORES

What they do well:
- They have frequent sales and end-of-season markdowns.
- They offer free seminars on different aspects of gardening during the spring and summer months.
- Facilities usually provide appropriate shelter for

plants (shade structures, sometimes drip irrigation for hanging plants, etc.)

- The most common, hardy plants are offered, but these stores also provide a variety of other plant choices.
- There may or may not be trained staff available to answer questions.

Watch out for:

- Older plants may have pests and diseases. Usually these stores routinely pitch or drastically reduce the price of weak, diseased, and pest-ridden plants. Sometimes these plants can be revived, but often they are past the point of no return.
- Scrutinize all plant tags. Make sure the perennials are truly perennial in your area.

THE SPRING "SUCKER CROP"

Resist buying summer annuals too soon in the spring, even if they've arrived at stores. There's little to gain by planting them too early. The days may be warm, but the plants can still be hit by morning frost, and while cool weather may not kill them, they won't grow. In fact, they may actually become stunted or experience delayed growth compared to plants installed after the weather warms up. The tip-off that it's too early are "protect from frost" signs posted near the sale rack. If you're not sure of the last average frost date for your region, call your local county extension agent or wait for the signs to be removed. The stores lose nothing by selling to you twice—first when it was too early and a second time to replace everything that failed.

FULL-SERVICE NURSERIES AND INDEPENDENT GARDEN CENTERS

These stores pay attention to two very important things:

- **The plants.** They offer a wide assortment of annuals, perennials, bulbs, vines, shrubs, and trees grouped together by cultural requirements. Many nurseries also propagate plants on site, which means plants are grown in the local climate and appropriate for your region. The plants receive lavish attention. The experienced staff is knowledgeable in recognizing and treating pests, and they routinely deadhead, feed, and repot overgrown plants. Many nurseries are willing to handle special-request orders and locate unusual or hard-to-find plants. Some will even replace plants that did not succeed in your garden, but be sure to ask about this before you buy.

- **The staff.** Nurseries generally hire educated, knowledgeable people. It's one of the reasons you can expect to pay more for your plants, but then they're providing a valuable resource. Professional plant and

---

LATE SUMMER COLOR

Is your garden beautiful in the spring and lackluster later on? One easy way to get late summer color is to shop in the late summer. Just reserve a few bare areas around the flower bed when you're planting in the spring. Then when your garden is most boring, visit your favorite store or nursery and fill in those empty places.

nursery people are on hand to help you select the right plant for the right place. All you have to do is walk in with enough information for them to help you. Nurseries and garden centers also sometimes offer seminars, master gardener clinics, and news-letters.

Watch out for:

- You may unwittingly enlist the help of a Garden Evan-gelist. Questions regarding low-maintenance plants should be carefully phrased, as low maintenance may not mean the same thing to them as it does to you. Be specific!
- It's likely you'll pay more here for the same plants that are stocked by home improvement and discount stores. If you're looking for a plant you know well, there might not be any reason for you to shop at a nursery. The main difference between the same plant at these two types of stores is the care it receives after it's on the shelf.
- As with the other venues, check plant tag accuracy if the plant has been trucked in from afar. Some nurser-ies have signs posted beside the plants explaining care and the hardiness of the species. They'll usually tell you if the plant can make it through the winter.

ARBORETUM, MASTER GARDENER, SPECIALTY PLANT SOCIETY, AND GARDEN CLUB SALES

What they do well:

- These sales usually offer great bargain prices. They have no way to hold plants over to sell the following year, and prices reflect the impetus to sell everything. Their goal is to raise funds and send you home with lots of plants.
- Plants frequently come from the members' own gardens or are purchased especially for the sale. Generally this means they will be well adapted to your region. Often you can get interesting care instructions if the members aren't overwhelmed with shoppers.
- If you want a hard-to-find species, arboretum and specialty plant society sales are good places to shop.

Watch out for:

- Plants often vary in quality, depending on the group holding the sale. If they've been freshly dug up, try to get them in the ground immediately. If you can't, keep them in bright or filtered shade until you can.
- Because these sales are often popular and crowded, it can be difficult to get questions answered if the event is understaffed.
- Beware of Garden Evangelists who might encourage you to buy a plant that doesn't suit your gardening style.

Mail Order and Catalogs

What they do well:
- Seed and plant catalogs put a wide variety of plants at your fingertips.
- A few even have pictures of emergent seedlings so you won't pull the wrong plants out when weeding.
- Sometimes the catalog itself is so educational it's worth keeping.

Watch out for:
- After their shipping experience, most plants will need tender care to settle in your garden.
- Photographs rarely show the entire plant and tend to emphasize only the best parts. If you're not familiar with what you ordered, it could turn into a big surprise in a few years, which could be good or bad, depending on your outlook. To get around this potential problem, check with your sources before ordering.

BULB BUYING

If you're choosing your bulbs from bulk bins, buy early in the season. That's the only way to know you're getting the bulbs you want. The longer you wait, the more likely it is other customers have inadvertently mixed them up. If you find yourself shopping too late in the season, get exactly what you want by buying bulbs in prepackaged bags.

ECONOMICALLY ADDING TO YOUR COLLECTION

Postbloom Bargains. Buy plants just past their peak blooming period. Many flowering shrubs are marked down soon after they've finished flowering. This is an affordable way to increase your plant collection, although you may not know the flower color until the next year.

Fall Bargain Hunting. Fall is an excellent time of year to put in perennials, shrubs, and trees. Fall planting ensures new growth as the ground warms in early spring (which may be earlier than you want to be out gardening!). Plus, many stores reduce plants at the end of the season since they can't keep them over the winter. Remember, though, that any plant you buy has spent the preceding growing season in a pot. Make sure it's not root bound, stressed, or diseased.

Bonus Plants. Look for a sixpack with seven plants, gallon perennials with two small plants instead of one, and so on.

Seeds. Starting from scratch is certainly an economical way to go, but seeds and seedlings need a lot of attention in the beginning. For more information on successful seeding see Appendix C, pages 164–166.

Native Plants. It's sometimes tempting to grab a shovel and dig up plants in the woods, but some species are protected and it's illegal to collect them on either public or private lands. To collect on public lands, many locales require you to obtain a permit from the managing agency. They can tell you which plants are protected. The best alternative to getting permits and practicing plant identification in the wild is to shop your local nursery. The bigger ones will carry gardenworthy native species, and any endangered species they offer will have been propagated by professionals for the retail trade.

Pass-Along Plants. Pass-along plants come from your neighbors and friends. There's a long-standing garden tradition which dictates you never say thank you for a pass-along. If you do, you may somehow jinx the plant. Instead, you're expected to share it with the next person who admires it. Whatever you do, be sure to plant it as soon as possible in growing conditions similar to those it came from.

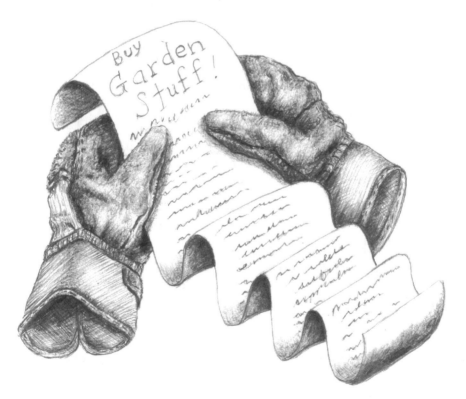

DOES IT MATTER WHAT KIND OF PACKAGING THE PLANT COMES IN?

If either saving money or jump-starting your garden is important to you, the answer is yes. Garden managers inclined to shop and garden in the late winter and early spring months will find a wide variety of packaging. When dormant, some plants can survive without soil or pots, and less packaging usually means a less expensive plant. Minimally packaged plants that haven't gone home with a shopper are eventually discounted or potted up.

Bare Root. Plants are sold as bare root in two very different conditions. Dormant, field grown trees, fruit trees, deciduous shrubs, roses and berries are available from midwinter to early spring. You'll recognize them on the sales floor in nurseries because their root systems are submerged in sawdust. Buy them while they are in sawdust, before the nursery has forced them into a pot, or has pruned the plant's root systems to fit into one.

The second condition for bare root plants are those that have had their root systems severely cut, bundled and wrapped for shipping. These plants will be stressed if new growth begins while they are packaged like this. Get them into the ground pronto.

Buying bare root plants has two clear-cut benefits for the consumer: they are cheaper, because shipping is simpler and no labor is expended in potting plants, and it's easy to inspect the root system.

Look for
- Healthy, symmetrical root arrangements
- Plump roots
- Enough roots to support the top growth

Reject

- Root systems with only two or three short stubs
- Roots that are black, mushy, withered, or brittle
- Plants that have begun to leaf out—they should have been potted some time ago

Ball and Burlap. Ball and burlap (B&B) trees and shrubs are dug from fields with their root systems intact. After the plant is lifted from the ground, the root ball is wrapped in burlap and secured at the base of the trunk with twine. The prime time to purchase, install, and plant B&Bs is in the spring, although these plants are available year round. It's often the only way large trees are sold.

Boxed Perennials. Hostas, dahlias, ferns, clematis, and bleeding heart are just a few of the plants sold in boxes in early spring. Boxed perennials are usually less expensive than potted plants. You're buying dormant root structures—roots, bulbs, corms, tubers, rhizomes. Inspect the root structure of any potential purchase to make sure you are getting the best plant.

Look for

- Firm and plump root structures sporting little root hairs
- Plants barely breaking bud—a little touch of green showing on the top of the plant guarantees viability

Reject

- Plants showing more than just a touch of green, straining to get out of the box—they're already stressed from lack of nutrients and soil
- Root structures that are withered or mushy

Pony Packs, Gallon Pots, or Flats. Time is the critical factor between the different container sizes—how much time you have before you want to see blooms and how long the plants have been waiting for you to buy them.

How soon do you need color in your garden? If your answer is, "I'm a patient person, I can wait," then use **pony packs** (pots with four or more young plants), an economical way to get annual bedding color in your garden. It will take them a little longer to bloom, but the difference could be negligible compared to 4-inch pots.

If your response is, "My in-laws are coming in a month," you should do well with **4-inch pots** or plants sold singly in small pots. These plants may already be blooming. You may find yourself planting them closer together for a bigger splash of color than you would get with one-gallon pots.

However, if you wail, "The dinner party is tonight—help!" you need **one-gallon pots** to provide instant color and gratification.

HOW DO I PICK OUT THE HEALTHIEST PLANTS?

Look for
- Plants with green, lush foliage
- Plants loaded with flower buds, not flowers. Like a soprano singing an aria at the Met, a plant in full bloom is treating you to a peak performance. And just as you wouldn't ask the soprano to sing at that level while hailing a cab, moving flowering plants also adds unnecessary stress. When a plant is in full bloom, all the energy and nutrients are channeled to the flowers. Catching a plant before it bursts out in

flower gives your plant a chance to settle in before it rewards you with a beautiful show.

- Plants with a pleasing shape. How does it look from a bird's-eye view? If possible, stand over it and look down on the plant. Are the branches evenly distributed around the base of the plant? Look for new growth ready to pop out. How does it look from the side view?

Reject

- Root-bound plants. Are roots pushing through drain holes in the bottom of the pot? Containers are only meant to be short-term homes for plants. If you find yourself with a root-bound plant, see the planting and transplanting section on pages 108–113.
- Tall and leggy plants. Again, it should have been transplanted to a larger pot long ago. Be prepared for a longer settling-in time.
- Dried-out, yellowed, wilted, mottled, or diseased leaves. You might be able to revive a dried-out plant, but bringing home a diseased plant is more work than it's worth.
- Insect damage. Look under leaves and check at the base of the plant. You'll just be adding more work if you accidentally bring these guys home.
- Damaged bark or limbs. Trees can be easily damaged during the shipping process. Check to make sure that the bark is intact and branches haven't been ripped or stripped from the trunk.

DECIPHERING "GARDENESE"

Some of the information printed on those tiny plant tags requires further amplification for successful plant tag gardening.

BOTANICAL NAMES

Botanical names provide you with clues about leaf or flower color, place of origin, or cultural requirements of the plant, helping you put the right plant in the right place. Plant names have two parts: The first name—the genus—is the big family name and the second—the species name—describes some unique aspect of the plant. For instance, all oaks are in the genus *Quercus*, so scarlet oak, which has outstanding red leaf color in the fall, was given the title *Quercus coccinea* because *coccinea* means "scarlet."

If you use botanical names, you'll be speaking an international language (like Esperanto for gardeners, horticulturists, and botanists). It doesn't matter if you're on the other side of the world, since the same plant has the same name everywhere. When you look for it at your favorite garden center, it can always be found by using the scientific name, even though the local or common name is different. Common names are more like nicknames; they're colloquial and often change from place to place. One plant may have several different common names, and several different plants may be labeled by the identical common name! Other plants never do get nicknamed and are always referred to by their botanical names.

Not all scientific names are true Latin; some are Greek, French, Japanese, and Arabic made to look like Latin. Others commemorate the first person to collect the plant. Knowing what the words mean may help you decide if a plant is going to measure up to your needs. However, this knowledge is best used as a guide, particularly when it comes to words indicating color. The feature described by the name may not be the feature you expect. For example, a plant with large yellow flowers, but large white leaves, might be named *alba* after the leaf color. Unless you become an expert in plant names, double check the information before buying

The following are a few examples of the words used in scientific botanical names with their meanings included so you can see how and why it works. Following is a sampling of botanical names.

Place Names. These are names that refer to the first place a plant was collected or where it is commonly found:

> *Arvensis, campestre,* and *pratensis* refer to fields and meadows. Plant in sunny open places.
> *Rupestre* and *saxatilis,* refer to rocky sites, *tectorum* to roofs, and *collina* to hills. Plant in places with quick or sharp drainage.
> *Palustris* means "swamp" and *ranunculus* means "frog." Plant in wet environments.

Size and Growth-Habit Words. These words are included in the name if the size or growth habit is worth noting:

> *Reptans, pumila, procumbens,* and *supina* describe creeping, low-growing plants. Usually these are groundcovers, or plants that function as groundcovers.

Compactus, densum, nana, and *reducta* all refer to a diminutive size.

Dendron is Greek for "tree." Plants with this word as a root are trees themselves or exhibit treelike qualities.

Fruiticans doesn't mean the plant has lots of fruit, it means shrubby and is used to describe plants dense with branches and foliage. These plants can be useful for screening and privacy.

Scandens is used to describe plants with a climbing habit.

Descriptive Words. These words describe a distinct feature of the plant such as color, size, shape, or scent of the flower:

Florida means "flowering" not "from Florida." A plant with this name indicates that it displays beautiful flowers.

Fragrans means "fragrant," which may be obvious, but you may be glad to know up front that *foetidus* and *graveolen* mean "stinking."

Stellata means "starlike" and usually describes a flower shape.

Heli is a root word for "sun." Plants with *heli* in their name may have color reminiscent of the sun (golden, yellow, orange), and/or brilliant sepals radiating from the center. These plants all do well in a sunny location.

Poly is Greek for "many." This could be "many" of just about anything—leaves, stamens, flowers.

Hirta, mollis, and *trichos* all mean "hairy"—usually on the stems, leaves, or branches. Plants with these words in their name may have a higher tolerance for periodic drought or more sunlight than other plants in their genus. That is not to say that they are all sun-loving, drought-tolerant plants, but the hairs help them retain moisture and protect plant tissue from otherwise scorching sunlight.

Carpa is one botanical term for fruit. When you find *macrocarpum* in the name, you can be sure the fruit is unusually large for the genus. This may be good to know if you don't want a yard littered with big, big fruit. *Xantho* before *carpa* means yellow fruit. This could be a very desirable trait, especially if it refers to a berry that persists on bare winter branches.

Vulgaris is the most commonly found variety of that species.

The following color words are used to describe just about any part of the plant. Frequently, it's the flowers, but if there are plant parts with unusual colors, that may be the feature referred to in the name.

alba, candida, leuco—white
azurea, carulea, cyan—blue
citrina, flava, lutea, xantho—yellow
coccinea—scarlet
discolor—two colors
ionantha, purpurea—purple/violet
niger—black
rhodo, rubrum—red
sanguinea—blood-red
viridis—green

"In Honor Of. . . ." Many plant names commemorate botanists, horticulturists, explorers, royalty, and even family members. The names are latinized before they are used. For example:

> *Clarkia,* after Captain William Clark, 19th century explorer
>
> *Lewisia,* after Captain Meriwether Lewis, 19th century explorer
>
> *Davidia,* after Armand David, French missionary, 19th century plant collector in China.

INTERPRETING PLANT TAGS AND GARDEN LINGO

There really isn't an industry standard as to the exact meanings of certain words. The following list is offered as a general guideline for some of the words used to describe sun and soil requirements. They can't always be given in measurable quantities, so you'll have to rely on observation to make a match.

Sun and shade

Full sun—nothing less than six hours of unimpeded sunlight.

Partial sun or partial shade—as the sun moves through the yard, the bed in question is in both full shade and full sun sometime during the day.

Sun/partial shade—the plant does best in sun but can take partial shade.

Partial shade/sun—the plant does best in partial shade but can take some sun.

Dappled shade—sunlight peeks through in various spots during the day, such as the areas under deciduous trees.

Filtered shade—could be called light shade or bright shade as well. Sun is reflected into the area causing some brightness, but it remains shady most of the day.

Full shade—no sun penetrates the area. It's dark with no reflection to brighten it, as under evergreen trees.

Condition and moisture content of soil

Rich in organic matter—deep rich soil, high in organic matter, or well-prepared soil. Naturally loamy soil or soil that's heavily enhanced with conditioners (animal manure, compost).

Low fertility levels—soil more towards the fringes with no conditioners or loam added.

Wet—boggy, marshy, standing puddles.

Moist, dampness—soil doesn't completely dry out between watering, but there is no standing water.

Well-drained, good drainage, adequate drainage—water moves through the soil slowly enough to completely moisten it and then drains off.

Quick-drained or sharp-drained soil—water passes through soil immediately, as in rocky, sandy, hillside, or alpine conditions.

Dry—soil retains no moisture.

GETTING DOWN AND DIRTY

PLANTING YOUR GARDEN

Planting is a recurrent garden activity. The day may arrive when you want to add fresh faces, move plants around, or divide and replant perennials. If you're going to make the effort, here's how to make sure the results are successful.

THE IMMUTABLE LAWS OF PLANTING AND TRANSPLANTING

- Setting plants out under the hot sun in dry dirt is a recipe for disaster. For successful planting and transplanting, recreate a spring day. While cool, overcast, and damp weather may not be the most pleasant gardening conditions, they're ideal conditions for planting and transplanting. Sometimes you have no choice, or misty weather isn't forecast. What do you do? Luckily, there are ways around hot, dry weather. To lessen plant stress wait until the end of the day, when shade covers the new location. Let the plants spend their first few hours in your garden out of the sun and heat to give their systems a chance to adjust.

- It's best to move around plants when they're dormant. This is especially true for larger shrubs, trees, and roses. (Most plants enter dormancy in the fall and break dormancy sometime in the spring.)

- Whether you're planting in the ground or in a pot, never move from dry dirt to dry dirt. No exceptions. Thoroughly water both the plant and the soil in the new location.

- Dig a hole in the new location. It should be wider but not much deeper than the root ball of the plant you're moving. If you're digging among established

ARE THEY WEEDS OR ARE THEY FLOWERS?

How can you tell if you've got a weed or a flower seedling popping up? Before you lovingly encourage weeds to grow all over your garden, you'll have to do a little investigative work to decide if they're weed babies or not. Are the same seedlings distributed all around the yard? Then most likely they're weeds. Look at the plant nearest the seedlings. Do the leaves match? Could they be offspring? If there is only one set of leaves, you'll have to wait awhile because the first set of leaves aren't the "true" leaves. They bear no resemblance to the mature leaves of the plants they will become. Hopefully, when the second set emerges above the first, you'll recognize them. If you do, you're in luck. If you don't, your alternative is to wait and watch. You may have to wait until it flowers to decide if it's a weed. If it turns out you don't want it as a member of your plant community, you've learned something for future reference. Just be sure to pull it before it sets seeds.

plants in your garden, put the dirt from your hole into a large pot or bucket as you dig. Once the new plant is in place, gently dump the soil back in around it. This saves trampling and damaging the adjacent plants. If the soil in the new spot is compacted, the plant will do better in a bigger hole. Otherwise, the roots will hit the sides of the hole and wind around it as if they were in a pot. Break up the compacted soil before putting it in the hole. If possible, mix it with looser soil from other areas of your garden or add a soil conditioner (see pages 127–128).

- When transplanting from the garden, your main objective is to disturb your plant's root system as little as possible. First, thoroughly soak the plant (this can even be done a few hours before digging). Soaking keeps the soil intact around the roots. Then, take as much of the root ball as possible, digging to the outside perimeter of its foliage (known as the dripline). It's not always possible to dig that far around a plant, especially when you're thinning out an overgrown area of your garden. If you don't manage to get a lot of the roots, trim down the top of the plant. A smaller plant is easier for a smaller root system to sustain, so it will suffer less stress.

- When transplanting from a plastic pot, thoroughly soak the plant to keep transplant shock to a minimum. If the pot is two gallons or less, support the plant at the base of the stem with one hand, then turn the pot upside down and loosen it. Rather than pulling the plant out of the pot, pull the pot off the plant. If the pot is over two gallons, tip the pot on its side. Gently rock it back and forth, putting pressure on the side as you do. Pull the plant out by the base of the stem. If a tug-of-war ensues, cut the pot! Loosen the potting soil around the outside edges of the root ball before plunking it in the ground. If it's root bound, you're going to have to cut the roots and spread them out so they can seek out water and food. At this point the plant is already so stressed you'll be helping it. Essentially, you're root pruning and it'll actually stimulate new root growth.

- Toss in some slow-release fertilizer granules. You can also mix them with the soil you're returning to the hole.

- Put the plant in the hole and gradually replace the soil, firming it down every so often as you go. Tamp out any air pockets around your root system or the roots will freeze in winter because there is no insulating soil to protect them. Air pockets also cause roots to dry out faster and shrivel up in summer heat.

- When you're done, water the plant slowly. A quick drenching will wash out soil.

- Keep an eye on the plant for a few days. If it begins to wilt, a light sprinkle for a couple of hours in the early evening or morning to imitate April showers will really help. Try blocking the sunlight with an umbrella to offer relief. Sometimes it takes a few days, or a light rain, to revive a plant.

At first it may not seem as if you are creating the garden of your dreams, but as you've probably discovered, the garden of your dreams can end up being a nightmare to maintain. By utilizing the methods of garden tailoring, you can create a garden that is in harmony with you—one that looks good, and that you're willing and able to care for.

PART THREE

Garden Management

Gardening is like few other things you do, for you set in motion a web of activity that has no ending. A garden cannot exist without some form of management. You now know you can't just put something into the ground and walk away, trusting that Mother Nature will automatically take over. On rare occasions this approach works out, but more often than not, if you don't provide for your garden's needs and Mother Nature would prefer to have other plants ("weeds" to you), she will win out. Over time, your design won't stand much of a chance without your intervention. On the other hand, as your interest develops or wanes, you'll alter the garden to suit your circumstances.

This section of the book involves the "getting out and doing" part of gardening that keeps your personal vision and design work intact over time. Sure, it's a nuts and bolts kind of information to give you the know-how, but more importantly, it gives you the "know-whys"—why you do the chores to keep your garden going. Sometimes understanding the "whys" involved will spur you on when your interest in the actual task is nil. You'll be more effective at whatever level of involvement you choose.

EXPLAINING GARDEN MANAGEMENT

Garden management occurs in three arenas. So far you've read about the "what is" category—acknowledging nature's unchangeable dictates. And you've learned to choose plants appropriate to your site and your personal style. Part three completes the picture by showing you how to maintain those plants, covering basic garden practices and describing how to tackle garden chores. This enables you to prioritize chores to make the biggest impact on your garden, or the least impact on you, depending on your needs at any given time. The goal is to boil everything down to what absolutely has to be done and what you can let go.

To begin with, forget about having to control everything. Total control is impossible. Management is all a gardener really can do. The garden shouldn't be perceived as a war zone, with you pitted against Mother Nature. You'll never win! As long as you think you're locked into some kind of combat, you'll perpetuate the notion that you can do things your own way and somehow be successful. There are always bigger influences at work. There is one overriding rule that governs garden management: a gardener begins with what is true about nature and then facilitates or hinders what occurs.

INTERACTING WITH MOTHER NATURE

As a gardener, the one area you *do* control is deciding how to interact with Mother Nature to maintain your garden. It's never a static relationship between Mother Nature, the gardener, and what the gardener has created. Gardeners work with or against the natural processes.

It's most efficient to work along with, or *enhance*, the natural processes already at work. For instance, you can learn to recognize when your flowering shrub or vine is producing its buds for the next year. Prune at the right time and you'll be the recipient of many flowers. Prune at the wrong time and you'll have few or none.

Sometimes gardeners work against, or *thwart*, natural processes to the gardener's advantage, but thwarting natural processes is tool-intensive and usurps more of your time. If you decide to create a laurel hedge, for instance, you'll have to prune frequently to keep it the size and shape you want. English laurel is really a tree and forcing it into a hedge thwarts its normal tendencies.

How Gardeners *Enhance* the Work Mother Nature Already Does

The easiest way to save yourself extra effort in the garden is to work along with the natural order of things. The following concepts will save you work by taking advantage of what's already happening.

Use plants native to your region. There are a great number of plants already perfectly adapted to your climate, requiring far less attention from you than nonnatives. Many are practically maintenance free! You'll be less plagued by disease and insect troubles using plants that have already developed strategies to fight off the indigenous pests. If you want to use native species, inquire at a nursery to find out which are "gardenworthy." Just because you can find it out in the woods doesn't mean it should be in your garden. In fact, if you can find it in a nursery that's a clue it might be worth having. Gardenworthy plants are ones that mind their manners (they don't reseed like crazy or bring in unwanted pests and diseases), have at least one outstanding (and desirable) physical feature, and look good in your design.

Mulch to enhance your soil. By maintaining tidy flower beds free of fallen branches and decaying leaf litter, you actually interrupt the natural decomposition process. Spreading a layer of organic mulch (bark, pine needles, manures—see pages 129–130) replenishes what growing plants take out of the soil.

Consider a plant's rate of growth. When you give plants enough room to grow without interference, you're working with Mother Nature. As your garden's creator and manager, you choose whether or not to locate a plant in a spot with enough room for it to reach its eventual mature size. If you take into consideration a plant's growth rate, you save yourself work. Their rate of growth affects how quickly some plants will overshadow their neighbors in a flower bed, depriving them of the sun and nutrients they need to thrive.

Prune to stimulate growth. In this case, pruning encourages the plant's natural inclination to flower and produce vigorous growth. A cut made at the right spot, at the right time of year, channels a plant's energies, intensifying its readiness to burst forth (roses are a prime example of this).

How Gardeners *Thwart* Natural Processes to Their Advantage

When you thwart natural processes, you prevent Mother Nature from redesigning your landscape. Your yard is brought into conformity with your personal ideals of beauty.

Weed to disrupt the "survival of the fittest" scenario. When you weed, you're removing highly successful plants perfectly suited to the spot they're invading. If you want to have a truly natural look, just let these plants multiply. Chances are, though, you're much more interested in maintaining something that isn't quite as ideally situated—or it would also be multiplying. If you don't control this evolutionary process, your more "desirable" plants will be crowded out.

Prolong a plant's natural life cycle. Supplemental watering, feeding, and pest control are ways gardeners alter this continual process of change. These simple acts, which most of us perform at one time or another, could be considered enhancing nature, but since your goal is to keep the plant from reaching the end of its natural life span and entering into the next stage—decomposition—you are actually thwarting Mother Nature.

Thwart the plant's desire to stop blooming. Your intent is to unnaturally prolong the bloom period. A flower's job is to ensure the continuation of the species by attracting pollinators and then going to seed. Gardeners, on the other hand, are primarily interested in making the colorful show last as long as possible. Bloom can be extended in two ways: by over-stimulating flower production with fertilizers and by postponing seed production through deadheading. When you neglect either of these activities, plants cross into the point-of-no-return and stop flowering.

Prune to alter natural forms. If you need to thwart the effects of time to achieve the look you want, you have more work to do. Whenever you trim things into tidy, geometric shapes, you're working against the plant's natural inclination to spread or fan out, and that requires maintenance.

Prune to keep plants healthy. Cutting out the dying parts on plants interferes with the normal progression of plant succession. In the wild, dead branches or twigs become open invitations to bugs and parasites. By trimming off the dead stuff, you're actually prolonging the life of the plant, postponing the beginning of the decomposition process.

TOOLS MAKE IT A GARDEN

A garden is maintained, and comes into existence in the first place, through the use of tools. Since what humans do is tend their collections of plants, the whole endeavor is made easier with tools. The plants in your garden will evolve at a different rate than those in the wild because they are subjected to the human activities of tending, managing, and using tools.

Whenever you're engaged in any of the five categories of gardening chores—cutting, weeding, hauling, watering and digging—just a few basic tools speed up the pace considerably. If you buy only a few tools per chore, the following list is prioritized to give you the most bang for your bucks and effort.

CUTTING

Hand pruners are used for cutting branches up to a half inch in diameter.

Loppers are great when leverage is needed to cut through larger branches or when branches are out of reach of your hand pruners.

A *pruning saw* is perfect for cutting off branches that are too large for your loppers.

Pole pruners are used to get at branches that are far above your head—useful for mature trees.

WEEDING

A *hand cultivator*, also known as a claw or hand rake, is the workhorse in the flower bed. Scraping the surface

of the soil with it dislodges as many weeds as possible.

Hoes can't be beat when you don't want to kneel to weed. Two favorites are the stirrup hoe (also called the hula-hoe or push-pull hoe) and the garden hoe.

A *dandelion weeder* has all kinds of nicknames, such as weed poker, asparagus weeder, or slug assassinator. This long, simple tool is ideal for leveraging out weeds with deep taproots.

HAULING

Five-gallon buckets are easier to haul around the yard when weeding and aren't extremely heavy when full.

A *contractor's wheelbarrow* is deep, so it cuts down the amount of trips you have to make to get rid of debris.

15-gallon totes (pots) are useful when transplanting. Many trees and large shrubs are sold in pots this size. They have handles on the side for easy lifting.

WATERING

Watering cans come in endless varieties. A "rose" (the end part resembling a tiny colander) attached to the spout keeps water from gushing out and washing away soil in pots.

A *jet-type hose attachment*, with a wide variety of settings, will be a boon when you need to mist seedlings or divided perennials, and for fertilizing.

A *soaker hose* is preferable to a sprinkler in a flower bed. It does a better job with less adverse effects. Water oozes out of the hose and goes straight to the root zone.

DIGGING

A *trowel* is an indispensable tool for planting small starts in flower beds and container gardens. Because trowels are constantly in use, it pays to have a good one. Cheap ones bend in hard soil.

A *garden shovel* is handy in flower beds, for edging and for weeding large areas. Sometimes called a floral shovel, it has a smaller blade than a regular shovel. The blade comes to a point in the middle, instead of being flat-edged.

A *large shovel* is necessary when digging holes for trees and bigger shrubs.

A *spading fork* isn't essential, but it's helpful for turning compost, breaking up soil, transplanting, and lifting soil.

SOIL—MORE THAN THE DIRT YOU WALK ON

Dirt's dirt, but soil grows things. Soil occupies its own ecological niche in the larger scheme of things. Good soil nurtures healthy plants. It's a medium brimming with lively insects and microorganisms hard at work.

Soil types come from varying combinations of two ingredients: humus (dead and decaying organic materials) and minerals (disintegrated rock). The spectrum of soil types runs the gamut. At one end is sand with coarse, loose mineral granules and no humus. If you try to hold it loosely cupped in your hands, it just falls through your fingers. It has no water-retentive properties. At the opposite end is clay, composed of tiny mineral granules too slick to let any

POTTING SOIL

Most potting soils bagged up for sale contain little or no actual soil. They can be chock full of any combination of peat, sand, compost, perlite, vermiculite, manure. When soil is included, it's been baked at high temperatures to kill any seeds, damaging bacteria, diseases, or preying insects lurking around. However beneficial microbes that help make nutrients available to your plant's roots have also been wiped out. There won't be any trace minerals and other nutrients available either. This means it's up to you to add fertilizer. Without this assistance, your plants are getting absolutely nothing.

organic materials enter, much less allow water and air movement. When water does manage to finally seep in, it often drowns plants by suffocating their roots. In the middle of the soil spectrum lies loam. It has a balanced mixture of mineral sizes and a high organic content. Water makes it to the root zone and stays long enough for plants to take up nutrients. Roots are able to wind their way through the soil and anchor the plant.

Luckily, most people have soils somewhere around the middle of the spectrum. It's the extremes that drive people crazy because there are a limited number of plants that can survive in those soils. To discover your soil type, try the easy test found in part two, pages 30–31.

ENHANCING THE SOIL YOU'VE BEEN DEALT

Does soil make that much difference? It definitely does if you're gardening at the fringes of the soil spectrum (clay or sand), and you'd like to increase your plant palette. For the majority of gardeners, it's a matter of choice whether to amend your soil or not. Indigenous plants from your area are already well adapted to it, so you don't have to change it to accommodate them. But other plants have developed their own tastes in soil, just as they have specific sun and water preferences. Amending soil just gives you the option to go in more directions. Conditioning, aerating, and mulching are three ways to amend soil. You can do one, all three, or none—and plenty of people don't do anything. But they're the kinds of things that provide a nice future return on your investment. They impact the "invisible" part of the plants, benefitting the parts above the ground that you love to look at.

Conditioners: Beef it Up

Soil conditioning happens naturally. In the woods, falling leaves and needles continually cover the ground (becoming mulch). In the process of decomposing they're worked into the soil by wildlife and weather (further breaking

---

STARTING OVER—HAULING IN TOPSOIL

Sometimes you just want to start over or, as is the case with many new homes, the property has been scraped down to hardpan. Try this simple formula for adding topsoil.

Soil Sundae—The recipe is easy, but the labor is back-breaking!

1. Dig into your existing soil a minimum of two feet (consider your existing soil as the ice cream).

2. Put down a layer of topsoil and mix with the native soil (the syrup).

3. Spread the remaining topsoil over this mixture (the whipped cream).

You should end up with a top layer of really nice topsoil, a layer where topsoil and native soil are mixed, and then your original soil. If you just fill the hole with topsoil and neglect the mixed layer, the change between the topsoil and native soil layers may be too abrupt, and the plant roots will hit the native soil like a wall. The plants will deplete the nutrients in the topsoil, plus have no way to anchor themselves, becoming a blow-over hazard.

---

down into conditioners), slowly renewing the soil. When you deliberately add conditioners to your flower bed, you'll be imitating Mother Nature—but speeding up the process.

Conditioners improve soil texture, add nutrients, and remedy compaction. (Compaction is when water puddles on top, but the soil underneath is dry.) The best conditioners are organic—manure, peat moss, compost—but there are other choices. Although it's fast and easy to buy conditioning materials bagged, many are also sold by the cubic yard. And you don't have to spend money if you're willing to compost. Simple compost how-to's are in Appendix B.

When you are preparing a new bed for planting, spread your conditioner out in a one and a half inch to two inch thick layer. Turn the conditioner completely into your existing soil with a spade, fork, or rototiller. It can be pretty hard to figure out how much conditioner to buy when you're standing in front of the bags at the home improvement store. Fortunately, you can't add too much when using organic conditioners. If you find you've brought home more manure or compost than you want to bother with, never fear—they make an ideal mulch for established beds.

When you add conditioners to an existing bed, be careful not to damage the delicate surface roots of well-established plants. To minimize this risk, spread a one and a half inch to two inch layer of conditioner around the plants and work it in gently over time as you weed and scratch in fertilizers. Doing this in sections around your yard every couple of years will maintain the garden soil's viability.

AERATION: FLUFF IT UP

While the physical labor of adding a soil conditioner may not be fun, you're accomplishing two tasks at once: conditioning and aerating. Twice the benefits! Aeration (adding air) naturally results from stirring up the soil. To understand the benefit of air, consider the difference between hardtack and white bread. Both use the same ingredients, wheat and water, but the first is hard and tough, and although people can eat it, it's not an enjoyable experience. However, when you add yeast to get air into the dough, it makes the dough lighter and the end product easier to cut. This is similar to what happens when air is worked into soil. Oxygen, water, and roots can then move freely through this looser medium. In nature, this is the work of earthworms—the consummate aerators. If only we could duplicate their work!

Mulch: Cover it Up

Mulch, a protective blanket you apply over your topsoil, makes gardening easier. It's another one of those things a gardener doesn't absolutely *have* to do, but the payoffs far outweigh the effort. Choosing your mulch material is a matter of personal preference. It should satisfy both your aesthetic needs and your desire to lighten the work load.

Physical and aesthetic benefits of mulch

- **Retains soil moisture.** You'll water less on hot summer days because the mulch cuts down on evaporation, preventing plants from drying out completely. Consistent moisture enhances root growth and helps roots grow deeper to better support the plant.
- **Insulates.** A layer of mulch protects the roots of those plants not adapted to either freezing or hot, baked soils.
- **Improves the topsoil.** An organic mulch will break down into a soil conditioner once it's mixed in.
- **Thwarts weed seeds from sprouting.** You receive the physical benefits of less bending and

the aesthetic benefit of more time for lounging in a chaise, admiring your garden.

- **Makes weeding easy.** If a weed or two manages to germinate and grow through your mulch cover, they stand in contrast to the mulch, making them easier to find and yank out.
- **Increases tidiness.** Flower beds look tidy and attractive with practically no weeds poking through.

Organic mulches such as aged bark, manure, peat moss, compost, grass clippings, hay, or nut shells are applied the same way you apply conditioners in an established flower bed. They are not a one-time fix, because organic mulches need to be replenished every so often, depending on how quickly they break down. When you reapply mulch, you're constantly renewing the soil. Use the same rule of thumb as conditioner—up to two inches is plenty. A very thick layer of over three inches of organic mulch creates more problems than benefits. Your plants could suffer a host a problems, from rot to suckering. In this case, more is not better.

On the other hand, inorganic mulches, such as plastic tarps or weed-cloth, are buried an inch or two below the soil surface. Gravel or rock used as an inorganic mulch is laid on top of the surface. If you decide to rearrange plants later, using plastic tarps and weed-cloth forces you to get out the scissors. Additionally, the plastic has a way of working its way closer and closer to the surface. With gravel and rocks, the problems work in the opposite direction. If your flower bed gets tromped on, or you dig around in it, the decorative gravel will eventually work its way down into the soil.

WOOD CHIP WARNING

Fresh bark or wood chips are better used on paths, not garden beds. While decomposing, they're greedy nitrogen feeders and steal nitrogen from any source, causing nearby plants to yellow and look pathetic. You're left with two choices. Either remove all the bark and wood chips or mix in fresh grass clippings (or bring in another source of nitrogen). If you like the look of bark, try aged bark. It's already partially decomposed and won't deplete the soil.

FERTILIZER: FOOD TO GROW ON

Feeding your plants is another matter of personal preference—whether you choose to fertilize or not, when you'll do it, and what you'll use. The majority of plants can get by without any supplemental feeding. "Get by" is the operative phrase here. They may be just fine without it, but when you fertilize, you increase the likelihood that plants will live longer and produce more flowers.

And here's the real clincher: They'll be less attractive to pests and diseases, and better able to protect themselves. This is the reverse of what you'd expect to happen! Healthy plants look attractive to us, so it stands to reason that it would also be true for bugs. But in this case, beauty is only in the eye of the beholder. Wimpy, droopy and forlorn plants rate a "ten" from a bug's perspective. They slurp and salivate over such an easy meal. Healthy (in other words, tough) stems aren't worth the effort. So in a roundabout way, you're accomplishing the same thing with fertilizer that you could with pesticides. The difference is you're not killing the pests, just holding them at bay.

What you use depends upon your gardening style and the plants you have. If you do decide to fertilize, you can select from chemical or organic, liquid or granular fertilizer. All fertilizers come with a recommended rate of application—seasonally, monthly, or weekly—and there are various methods of application to suit any gardening style. Depending on the fertilizer you choose, you might even be improving your soil texture.

Chemical or organic fertilizers?

Chemical fertilizers are a quick food fix for your plants—you get a lot of punch in a little bottle of precise formula. The basic plant nutrients have been distilled down to their essence and are delivered in liquid or a granular form. On the upside, they're widely available, aren't an assault to the olfactory nerves, are simple to store, and have enough styles of application to suit almost everyone. On the downside, they feed plants directly without enriching or building up the soil. They also tempt you to overfeed, and with fertilizer, more is not better. Overfertilizing damages both your plants and the soil.

Organic fertilizers—animal manure, composts, rock powders—feed your plants while actually improving soil fertility. When you use them you are making a long-term commitment to your soil. Bulky organic fertilizers have much lower concentrations of essential nutrients, and they take a fair amount of labor to apply and mix in, but they add immeasurable benefits. Plus, it's nearly impossible to overfeed with organic fertilizers. For more on fertilizers, see Appendix D.

HERE A SNIP, THERE A SNIP, EVERYWHERE A SNIP, SNIP

Pruning generally involves shrubs, roses, trees, and vines. Most garden managers discover that only a small number of their plants need frequent attention. Some plants need none, and the rest just require a tune-up every so often. Although entire books are devoted to this topic, a few basic principles will benefit all plants and serve you well.

Before you begin to cut your plants, two things must be said about tools. First, use sharp tools. Raggedy cuts take longer to heal and give pests more time to make inroads. Second, don't spread any diseases. If you find yourself cutting out diseased plant parts, clean your tool blade with an alcohol solution—rubbing alcohol works well—before cutting a healthy plant. Although this is a nuisance, if you don't you'll spread the very thing you're trying to eradicate. To simplify cleanup after pruning, lay a tarp down close to the plant you're working on. Throw your branches on it as you work, and then drag the whole kit and caboodle to your disposal site.

If pruning has left you confounded over the years, take heart; it is a skill that takes time to master, blending technique with artistry. The technique can be explained but the artistry lies in the eye of the beholder. You decide when you've cut enough. The best advice is to take your time, especially on older plants. Stroll around them. Scrutinize the shape. Check for any developing lopsidedness. When in doubt about where to cut, stop. You can always come back later and do more.

WHEN SUBTRACTION MEANS MORE— PRUNING TO STIMULATE GROWTH

There are the three places where new growth develops:

- **Branch tips**. When branch tips are pinched back, they put out bushy side growth.
- **Bud eyes**. To see what these look like, gently pull a leaflet off a major stalk. There will be a scar left behind. The little dot right above the scar is the bud eye. Cuts made directly above a bud eye cause new growth to pop out at that spot. Cuts made directly below them force the branch to die all the way back to the next bud eye.
- **Latent buds**. These lie hidden beneath the bark surface. No matter where you make a cut, new growth arises somewhere along the branch. Plants that respond well to shearing have latent buds.

WHIPPING YOUR PLANTS INTO SHAPE— PRUNING TO KEEP PLANTS HEALTHY

If all you ever remember are the following three objectives, you'll have mastered the most important aspects of pruning. Used as directed, they increase the life expectancy of your plants and forestall natural succession.

Objective 1: Remove dead stuff. Dead branches are targets for disease and pests. By removing them you take an active stance in prolonging the plant's life and block pests from completing the work of decomposition. First cut the dead stuff out and remove any branches that look practically dead with only a few leaves at hanging on the tips. Whenever possible, cut these branches at a crotch (the place where two branches meet) to reduce the number of unsightly stubs.

Objective 2: Remove potentially damaging stuff. Two rubbing branches will create a wound that turns into a bug and disease entrance. These are the next branches to go. Then take out any branches crossing close to each other. As they age and grow thicker, they can become rubbing branches or cause congestion.

Objective 3: Remove the congestion. Congestion in the center of your plant hinders air circulation, encouraging a host of diseases and bugs to take up residence. Insects have a jolly old time utilizing the easy traffic routes a snarled mess of branches provides. Have a dense center? Thin it out. Stumped as to where to begin? Pick a branch you think is a good candidate and visually follow it all the way down to the center of the plant. After you've traced it down to the largest, thickest branch, check to see whether the other branches connected to this main branch should also come out. If it's really tangled and impossible to see what's going on, grab the branch you want to cut and jiggle it. This gives you a better idea of all the smaller branches connected to it. Hopefully you'll be able to see what's at stake if you cut. If it seems like too much will come out, try another branch. There's no hard and fast rule about thinning, just trust your gut feeling. This is one of those things that, over time, you'll learn by doing.

DOES IT MATTER WHEN I PRUNE?

The time of year when you choose to prune will either stimulate or slow growth. In general, cool season pruning stimulates new spring growth. As soon as the air and soil warm up, those zesty buds lying in wait take off. Pruning in the middle of summer does not encourage the same surge of new branch growth as spring pruning. It began months ago; your plant is now occupied with the business of greedily grabbing all available nutrients to continue the spring surge. It's also either flowering or making seeds to ensure the continuation of the species. Summer is a good time to cut established hedges, for they won't put out the same amount of new growth as they would with a spring trim.

BEAUTY TREATMENT FOR TREES, SHRUBS, AND VINES

Single trunk trees

Keep in mind that when trees are small, any pruning you do influences how they'll look as they mature. Use Objective 2 when trees are small and easily handled with pruners or loppers. This will save you from having to deal with those same branches when they are thick enough to require a pruning saw. If everything in your tree is out of reach, it's time to call in professionals with the proper equipment, knowledge, and good insurance policies.

After your trees are well-established, you may find yourself contending with waterspouts and suckers. Waterspouts grow straight up from horizontal branches, making a 90 degree angle at the crotch. On fruit trees, these nonproductive branches use up nutrients that would be better utilized by branches supporting fruit Removing waterspouts from ornamental trees, though, is a matter of personal aesthetics. Thin, supple, whiplike branches growing at the base of some trees and shrubs are called suckers. They steal nutrients from the plant. When they grow from the trunk or directly below a graft, cut them off as close to the trunk as possible.

TREE TOPPING

Topping becomes an issue when the tree grows too large for its space or it blocks your view. Topping is not a natural thing to do and ultimately doesn't solve the problem because you are choosing a path that just creates more work. If you top for a view, you'll have to get up into the tree now and then to trim the additional bushy branches that will spring up. Even if you top a tree for safety reasons, it's possible to end up making it more hazardous. The tree can become unstable enough to be knocked over in a wind.

Remember that topping a tree is irrevocable; it will never have a natural tree shape again. If you do top, you should monitor the subsequent health of the tree. A hollow cavity or rot pocket can form where the cut was made, and when new branches grow from it, they'll have weak attachments to the trunk because of the rot pocket. These branches tend to break off, and can be very dangerous. Topping can also make a tree more prone to falling later, and, depending on the species of tree, topping can even kill it. Many trees will survive, though, if they have enough lower branches and leaves to make food. Never cut off more than 25 percent of the crown during one season, and don't remove too many limbs at once.

Shrub Shapes

Fountain or spout-like shapes. With some imagination, these plants might remind you of a whale spout, but they don't attain this shape for some time. These shrubs have numerous branches or trunks that pop directly out of the soil. Shrubs with this type of growth habit eventually need some extra attention. Although you may have kept up with the three pruning objectives, if the plant is over ten years old, it's safe to assume that the following pruning tune-up will rejuvenate it. This chore is best done over a three-year period. Your goal is to take out a third of the branches each year *at ground level*. Select the oldest branches, looking for those with the largest diameter. If you can't tell which are oldest, just make your best guess. Later that growing season the newly invigorated plant will sprout new branches. The following year repeat the process, again cutting back a third of the oldest branches. The third year finishes the job. During this time the plant will begin to regain vigor, producing more flowers. Its life span will even be prolonged.

Mounding shrubs. Plants in this category have numerous branches that originate from an area low on the main trunk, near ground level. In their youth they look very much like mounds. Of the Big Three, the first objective is all you really need to use. After removing the dead stuff, give them a yearly "haircut" to keep them in a mound-like shape. Without this annual shearing, they turn into gangly, awkward teenagers. If you do this to a spring bloomer right after it has finished, you'll guarantee flowers for the next year. In some cases it even encourages a second bloom during the same season.

The rest of the deciduous and broadleaf evergreen shrubs. There are many shrub forms; if your shrub doesn't match any of the descriptions listed above, give them the old 1-2-3. If you are concerned about flowers, read When Timing is Everything on pages 141–142.

Vines and climbers

Don't prune beyond objective one. If you take out rubbing and crossing branches or eliminate congestion you'll have no vine left! A wildly successful vine crammed into a place that's not big enough will force the garden manager to keep it in place with hand pruners and loppers. To short circuit unwanted surges of new growth, make your cuts in the summer by simply cutting back the longest canes to the spot where they join with other canes. However, when flowers are involved, consult When Timing is Everything before hauling out your cutting tools.

THE GARDENER AS SCULPTOR—
PRUNING TO ALTER NATURAL FORMS

Pruning to alter natural forms takes several guises. It happens when you cut plants vying for the same space, shape plants to please your eye, and make a hedge. At the farthest reaches are topiary, espalier, and pollarding.

Plants Vying for the Same Place

Sometimes when plants are young you may not have a clear idea of their growth habits and the actual shapes or sizes they will become. Then one day you notice you've got a jungle and something needs to give. At this point you must either prune or transplant. The latter is the wise choice.

If you leave plants in place and trim them to keep them in bounds, you'll still be pruning long after you could have dispensed with it all by transplanting.

Shaping to please your eye

Sometimes a few too many careless snips can lead gardeners down a pruning path they wish they'd never embarked on. The key to avoiding this dilemma is to take your time. Remember to step back every so often, making sure your cuts are achieving the look you desire. If you're not sure you're using the right tool, or how to make a cut, try out your best guess on a part of the plant that's hidden from full view. This way you can experiment without regrets. For example, you might contemplate pruning a favorite plant with hedge shears because they'll make quick work of the task. However, they cut branches indiscriminately and you aren't sure you'll like the results. Try a small test area, maybe even make a few cuts with your hand pruners for comparison's sake. You'll be able to see the best method to get your plant into the shape you want.

The growth habit and shape of a shrub or tree determines the best way to prune, but regardless of your long-term goals begin with the first three Pruning Principles. The best time to make pruning decisions is before you buy a plant. You should find out what you will need to do to maintain its shape. If you've already bought the plant, you still need to find out the same information befrore you get out the pruning shears.

Hedges

Shrubs considered as perfect hedge material have earned this status because they're full of latent buds. They fill in easily when cut, even when the cutting seems severe.

Beyond shaping, you only need to check for dead branches, which can be tough to spot because shearing forces these plants to become very dense in the center. In this case, congestion is the look you want! Keep a shaped hedge wider at the bottom than the top so all the foliage will receive sun and rain. (Don't confuse shaped hedges with hedgerows. Hedgerows are used as visual and physical barriers – often consisting of thorny plants allowed to grow into their natural shape.)

Topiary, espalier, pollarding

You've probably seen topiary, espalier, and pollarding being practiced without realizing what it was. Start any one of these methods of pruning and you have entered the realm of extreme pruning. It takes knowledge to get the beginning cuts right and requires frequent maintenance sessions to remain true to the shape you've imposed. Plants that look like a cone, box, dog, dinosaur or any other recognizable form are known as topiary, a very old pruning tradition.

Equally old is espalier which is the technique of training a plant (usually a fruit tree) onto a railing or trellis in a flat pattern. If you've ever noticed a tree that looks like it has pom-poms at the end of stubby branches, then you've seen a tree that has been pollarded. If you are intrigued by any of these, there are many excellent instructional books on these techniques.

When Timing is Everything— Pruning to Stimulate Flower Production

If you follow these guidelines, you'll never lose a season's worth of flowers from any plant. If you can't always follow the advice given, don't worry; your plant will survive and the flowers should return the following year.

Spring bloomers

These plants flower on branches formed the previous year. Prune immediately after flowering. Cutting branches for a vase may be all the pruning that's needed for plants such as lilacs and rhododendrons. Don't wait too long or you'll cut off flower buds forming for the next year's show.

Late spring and summer bloomers

Some plants flower on both the new growth of the previous season and the new growth of the current season. If you need to prune them, practice preventive maintenance pruning (à la *Pruning to Interrupt Natural Succession*) during the late winter. During periods of active growth, deadhead and groom. Roses especially benefit from such treatment.

Midsummer and fall bloomers

These plants flower on branches formed in the spring. They are best pruned in late winter or early spring before new flower buds appear. Summer flowering plants can handle a trim directly after blooming, but if you cut fall bloomers immediately after they've flowered, you run the risk of encouraging a certain amount of new growth, only to have it killed by early frost.

PINCHING

Chrysanthemums, fuschias, and marigolds are just a few of the plants that respond well to pinching. You can increase flower production in many annuals by giving them this treatment while they're young. By pinching off tender new growth at the ends of stems, you force new side growth from the bud eyes along the branch. This bushier plant in turn has more branches to produce more flowers. The younger the plant, the better this works, and it's best done on short branches before they start to elongate. Just use your fingers to squeeze off the tip down to a set of leaves.

PRUNING AND GROOMING HYBRID TEA ROSES

Hybrid tea roses have the most particular pruning and deadheading needs of all plants. Being a shrub, they can survive without being catered to, but they won't produce wave after wave of flowers if you ignore them. These roses are pruned for two reasons: to enhance flower production and to prevent disease.

Prune roses severely at the very beginning of spring to give them a healthy fresh start, and the first flush of flowers will be spectacular. You want to hit the period before they bud out, but after the last possible big freeze. In warm winter climates, prune in midwinter to help imitate a sorely needed dormant season. Rust, blackspot, and mildew thrive wherever there's poor air circulation, so maintaining an uncongested center is essential to the plant's health. It cannot be ignored.

If you can't bring yourself to prune severely, give your rose a good grooming, and you'll still have beautiful flowers, although not as many. If you have more than one rose bush, experiment a little. Give one the full treatment and lightly groom the others. You'll soon see the difference between a thwacking and a trim.

How to thwack a rose

1. Start, as always, with the three pruning objectives (pages 134–135).

2. Ideally, the center of the rose should be shaped like a deep vase. Your first cuts in the spring set up this shape. Always choose leaf scars on the outside of a cane, rather than on the inside of it, or you'll cause the new branch to grow towards the center of the plant. One of the most important things you can do for a hybrid tea rose during the growing season is to keep the center of the shrub open. Rust, black spot, and mildew thrive wherever there's poor air circulation, so an open center is essential to the plant's health. It should be almost sacred.

3. Make all cuts at a 45-degree angle, with the top of the cut on the same side of the leaf scar and just above it. The bottom of the cut ends on the opposite side of the cane as the leaf scar, but not below

it. It takes practice to get a feel for this, but once you learn to prune a rose, you can prune anything.

4. Go ahead, be ruthless. If you have crossing branches and one of them is growing towards the center of the plant, that's the one that should go. Cut your canes back to leaf scars around 18 inches from the ground, and try to keep the major canes all the same height. Getting your shrub down to three or four canes is good. They will look like a bunch of prickly sticks someone shoved in the ground, but honestly, roses do well cut back this far, and your rose will not need this kind of pruning again until next spring.

How to groom a rose

1. Deadhead down to a five-leaf leaflet or to leaf scars all season until fall.
2. Pick off diseased and discolored leaves before they hit the ground. If you're so inclined, you can also take off all the leaves within a foot of the ground to deter those nasty little disease spores lying in wait for a splash of water to bounce them back onto your innocent rose.
3. When you feel you're about a month away from the first frost, stop pruning and deadheading to let rose hips develop. Any new growth will have time to harden and your rose will be ready for winter.

Pruning roses gives you some control because you direct the growth and shape of the plant. You save yourself work by keeping it disease free. But perhaps you've decided now that these finicky roses won't mesh with your filters! You can still have roses; however, antique shrub roses and miniature roses might be a better match.

CONTROLLING CRITTERS YOUR WAY

There really aren't good bugs and bad bugs in nature; they become bad bugs to you when they're destroying your plants. Generally, if you have bugs, it's because a plant was in trouble in the first place. One of an insect's jobs is to hasten the decomposition process, so they're naturally attracted to plants teetering on the edge. Pests are similar to

the large predators in the wild. In the same way that wolves go after the weak, the old, or the young, so do bugs. It seems as if they should prefer the healthy green stuff, but that plant tissue is tough to burrow through. Most bugs find it much easier to attack whatever is dying, although some, such as aphids, are attracted to tender new growth.

There are many reasons a plant becomes stressed. Severe weather such as unseasonable cold snaps, drought, flood, hail, and wind can weaken an otherwise healthy specimen. Likewise, ignoring cultural requirements by planting in the wrong place can marginalize a plant. If it doesn't die quickly, it may spend a long time just sitting in your garden like a statue, waning imperceptibly for years. As it weakens, any plant pathogen lurking on the soil or sitting dormant nearby can readily gain a foothold if accidentally transferred to the ailing plant. A death spiral starts as it begins to succumb, sending out distress signals that set the stage for decomposition. Receptive bugs pick up the messages and go to work. In the wild, dead plants house bugs that in turn feed birds, or feed the frogs that feed birds . . . You get the picture. Because we usually strive for a sense of order and beauty in our gardens, we want to stop this process before it reaches the messy decomposition stage.

The more plants you have, the more potential insects you have. If these normally occurring bugs become pests in your garden, you can deal with them in two divergent ways. One approach, the "open" method, enhances natural processes, while the other, the "closed" method, depends heavily on man-made chemical solutions. Each method has its advantages and disadvantages, and it's even possible to mix and match a bit when dealing with a particular problem.

OPEN GARDENS TOLERATE PESTS

The holistic method of problem solving in your garden is known around gardening circles as Integrated Pest Management (IPM). You work to enhance and mimic what occurs naturally, cultivating a lively, open-ended ecosystem. Up and down the food chain, insects, birds, butterflies, frogs, and so forth, buzz in and out of a garden that remains open to them. Each link in this chain feeds upon another; when you eliminate one link you cause the others to go haywire. An open system strives to keep the chain intact. The challenge is keeping the welcome mat out, while at the same time ensuring that your garden doesn't get trashed. You have to act as a vigilant bouncer. This is inherently time- and labor-intensive, so you may choose to follow some, but not all, of the practices.

Components of an open garden

Put the right plant in the right place. Plants in the right place thrive. Plants in the wrong place or in marginal situations put out distress calls to bugs and are receptive hosts.

Remove plants that are constantly struggling to survive. When you remove a suffering plant, don't replace it with the exact same plant in that same spot. Either try a variety that is resistant to the attacking marauders or choose an entirely different kind of plant.

Use disease-resistant varieties whenever possible. Some regions are more prone to certain problems due to weather patterns or a lack of natural predators (such as a particular bird that feasts on a particular bug). You might not be able to have your first plant choice after all. Rather than feeling restricted, realize that by sticking to your filters, you'll get something better able to withstand the challenges of your site.

Be consistent about meeting watering needs. Although there are a few plants that can tolerate alternating drought and monsoon-like conditions, most plants suffer from such drastic treatment. Subjecting them to these continuous cycles weakens their stamina, sending them into the death spiral.

Use fertilizers to boost plant health. Again, healthy growing plants resist bugs and crud. Supplementing available nutrients with a good all-purpose fertilizer strengthens their ability to fend for themselves.

Don't let weeds win. When weeds get the upper hand, they can hamper air circulation, which in turn promotes diseases. Weeds can also harbor insects. Eliminate bug abodes, and you reduce their population.

Remove diseased, decaying, and dead plant parts. Close the pest restaurant. Prune out dead and dying branches. Rake up diseased plant material to prevent crud from overwintering on the soil, only to reappear in the spring. Plucking off affected leaves is another way to help halt the cycle. Whatever you do, don't compost diseased material, or you'll recycle the problem back onto your beds.

Accept a certain amount of bug dining. A little damage is okay. So a few leaves may get chomped—this is one of those battles you can never totally win. But having said that, major damage is not okay. You can either remove and replace the plant or, if you're willing to put forth the effort, start some kind of treatment.

When all else fails, treatment usually begins with gaining some knowledge—time to troop back to your resources with as many observations as possible to figure out the problem. This might also be the time to invest in another book diagnosing pest and diseases and suggesting solutions.

Although organic solutions can be labor-intensive, the answer to a pest problem can sometimes be as simple as removing the invaders by hand. A pest that is robbing your plants one year can be put under house arrest the next year with a few preventive measures. It's even possible to have an open system *and* use man-made chemicals. To accomplish this, treat only infested plants. Blanket spraying the entire bed will disturb the delicate balance between prey and predator that you've been encouraging.

If this advice goes beyond what you're willing to do, manufactured chemical solutions, as used in the closed method, could be the better answer for you.

CLOSED GARDENS BANISH PESTS

When you choose chemicals, you're using manmade poisons to keep insects and diseases out of your yard. These act as more than simple "No Trespassing" signs. Although they're designed to rid you of certain problems, they repel or kill many insects at once—even the good bugs that would prey on the bad bugs. Chemical sprays can't distinguish between "good" or "bad" bugs. As a result, there won't be much bug or animal activity in your garden as long as you use them. Although spraying gives threatened or marginal plants a chance to recover, no amount of spraying can remedy a plant put in the wrong place.

Chemical solutions are usually easy and quick, especially if you hire professionals to do the job. If you apply them yourself, keep in mind that more is not better. It's even possible to overdo it and destroy the very plants you're trying to help.

You have to spray regularly to keep your ecosystem completely closed to insects. A one-time application won't work if you continue to maintain plants that are sending out signals that attract bugs. The insects are a normal part of the environment at large. They will always be hovering nearby, going in and out of your neighbors' yards. The minute the spray wears off your troubled plant, the bugs return. For some larger infestations, unless everyone in your vicinity sprays, it's a wasted effort. In such cases, the natural processes at work are much larger than your yard, and you can't control them alone.

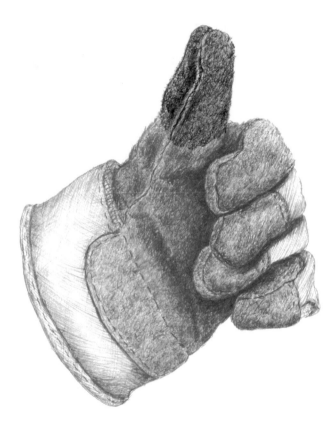

Pitiful No More

Many are the factors that send one down the path toward feeling brown thumbed and pitiful. Maybe it began with well-meaning gardening friends who couldn't fathom why you didn't want to be just like them. Or perhaps it started in your garden when you experienced one plant death after another, never understanding exactly why. Perhaps you have coaxed diverse plants from every corner of the planet to attempt to thrive side by side. Black-eyed Susans from the American prairies, lavender from the hillsides of France, and roses from China might or might not be good plot-mates in your particular gardening site.

Now that you've whittled the essence of gardening down

to a personal scale, you'll gain confidence as you encounter more success. When you become familiar with its underlying principles, the gardening realm seems much less like a mammoth enigma.

Opening this book was the first step in taking charge of your gardening experience. With the options laid out clearly before you, you're in control of your choices. They'll be true to you and your garden. Most importantly, you won't give up on yourself as a gardener, whatever form your gardening takes. You're pitiful no more.

Appendices

A. THOSE ONE (OR TWO) GOOD GARDEN BOOKS

Basic garden books

Gardening Basics. By Ken Beckett, Steve Bradley, Noel
   Kingsbury and Tim Newbury; John E. Elsley consulting
   editor. Sterling Publishing Co. Covers maintenance,
   design, and plants succinctly. Well illustrated, easy to
   understand. Favorites given in each plant category.

Sunset National Garden Book. By the Editors of Sunset Book
   and Magazines. Sunset Books, Inc., 1997. A well-
   organized gardening book, including plant lists, plant
   descriptions, and gardening basics. Clearly written and
   easy to understand.

Sunset Western Garden Book. By Sunset Publishing Corpora-
   tion, 1998. Every climatic zone in the western half of the
   U. S. nicely detailed making it easier to pick the right
   plant. Plant lists to satisfy many different site conditions, plant encyclopedia with brief descriptions,
   maintenance how-to included.

Gardener primers

Basic Gardening: A Handbook for Beginning Gardeners. By Louise Carter. Fulcrum Publishing, 1995. Focuses on the most basic techniques of gardening.

The First-Time Gardener. By Pattie Barron. Crown Trade Paperbacks,1996. Nicely illustrated basics book. Plant lists interspersed throughout.

Gardening for Dummies. By Michael MacCaskey. IDG Books, 1996. Gardening information imparted in an amusing, easily understood manner. Emphasis on gardening basics.

Plant encyclopedias

American Horticultural Society Flower Finder. By Jacqueline Heriteau, and Andre Viette. Simon and Schuster: A Stone Song Press Book, 1992. Lists by blooming season, site exposure, site niches, foliage effect, themed gardens.

The Easiest Plants to Grow Edited. By Jennifer Bennet, Ortho Books, 1996. Lists by plant type, size region or flower color. Short descriptive paragraphs include cultural requirements and problems.

Pick The Right Plant. By Time Life Books, 1998. Lists by sunlight exposure, then sub-lists by plant types.

Right Plant, Right Place. By Nicola Ferguson. Simon and Schuster Fireside Book, 1984. Listed by site conditions, plant type, and desired features. Cross-referenced.

What Plant Where. By Roy Lancaster. A DK Publishing Book, 1995. Very short lists (10-12 plants) with photos, cultural requirements, etc. First order of organization: Perennial, Climber, Shrub, Conifer, Trees. Further broken down into other criteria: fragrance, leaf coloration, site consideration, etc.

Books addressing specific kinds of plants, sites

100 Best Plants for The Coastal Garden. By Steve Whysall. Whitecap Books, 1999.

Roses. By Sunset Books Inc. Menlo Park, CA 1998.

Tough Plants For Tough Places. By Gary Vergine and Michael Jefferson-Brown. Contemporary Books, 1998.

What Perennial Where. By Roy Lancaster. DK Publishing, 1997.

Plant books to help you design

The Gardener's Book of Color. By Andrew Lawson. Reader's Digest, 1996.

Take Two Plants. By Nicola Ferguson. Contemporary Books, 1999.

Specialty books

Dead Snails Leave No Trails. By Loren Nancarrow and Janet Hogan Taylor. Ten Speed Press, 1996. Organic pest control.

Pruning Made Easy. By M. Lombardi and C. Serra Zanetti. A Wardlock Book, 1997. Well illustrated with clear photos and specific help for specific plants.

Rodale's Successful Organic Gardening Pruning. Rodale Press. 1995.

Secrets to Great Soil. By Elizabeth P. Stell. Storey Communications. Simple, easy to understand, heavily illustrated.

Regional books of lists

Taylor Publishing Company offers several regional books that have a fabulous array of lists to fill site or plant needs. The lists include only plant names, and are best used with a good plant encyclopedia. If Taylor does not publish one for your region, you might be able to find something similar that covers your area.

❧ B. COMPOST HAPPENS ❧

It's true, no matter what you do or don't do, your compost pile will shrink and decompose. Compost just "happens." Although your active participation can speed things up, it isn't required. You're merely the facilitator.

There are two methods of composting generally used, the outdoor compost bin and the worm bin. Outdoor bins handle yard waste, while worms in their little bins do amazing work with kitchen scraps. Why not mix your kitchen scraps in with your yard waste? The best reason is to keep vermin from lurking around the compost pile looking for spoiled, rancid treats. In fact, some municipalities regulate compost contents for this very reason.

THE BASIC INGREDIENTS

Regardless of the amount of time you want to spend getting your compost going, there are three basic ingredients of a working compost pile:
1. Green and brown waste
2. Moisture
3. Air

GREEN (FRESH) AND BROWN (DEAD) WASTE

Just as the words imply, green waste is green and brown waste is brown. Green materials are high in nitrogen, while brown materials are high in carbon. Examples of green waste include grass clippings, fresh leaves, weeds, and fruit and vegetable kitchen waste. Examples of brown waste include dead leaves, coffee grounds, dog hair, nut shells, and paper—any kind of shredded paper except carbon paper (no kidding, even colored magazine pages will get gobbled up).

In the spring and summer months, green material is plentiful, and when leaves begin to turn in the fall, brown waste is easy to come by. When the ratio between them is equal, each helps the other break down faster, making workable compost that much sooner. There's no need to be precise; just try not to overload one or the other. And even if you don't have both at the same time, you'll still end up with compost.

The thicker and bigger the material, the longer it takes to break down. You can hasten things along by chopping or shredding, but even if you don't bother, remember—compost happens.

Two cautionary notes:

- Avoid using animal by-products such as cheese, butter, ice cream, oil, meat—anything that could turn rancid. Foods cooked in oil are attractive to vermin, so you could find yourself running afoul of city codes.
- Don't put diseased parts of plants in your compost. It's tough for home composters to heat the pile hot enough to kill diseases. The pathogens will just live on in the compost, ready to attack once it is spread into your garden.

MOISTURE

You don't want your compost pile to be wringing wet. That's the route to a slimy, smelly mess. Yet if it's too dry, the worms can't survive and everything just sits there. The trick is to keep it slightly moist. Putting it in a sheltered place (such as under a tree canopy or eaves) keeps it from getting drenched during wet seasons (you can also throw a tarp over it). Then sprinkle the pile with water during dry spells.

AIR

There are two types of soil microorganisms at work in a compost pile—aerobic and anaerobic. When oxygen is freely available, aerobic conditions exist. Microorganisms working in aerobic environments release nearly odorless carbon dioxide and water as by-products. When a pile compresses and no oxygen is available, anaerobic conditions exist. Anaerobic piles are stinky, gloppy messes, because the end result of these decomposers is a gaseous form of nitrogen. You'll have an anaerobic pile by default if you fail to turn or aerate it. Using a pitchfork or spading fork for this job will save your back. If you have a small pile, poke holes in it with a big stick, a piece of rebar, or an aerator made especially for the job.

SOME LIKE IT HOT, SOME LIKE IT COLD

THE OUTDOOR BIN

Composters talk about two different kinds of piles, hot or cold. If it's not your style to hover over a compost pile, you'll like cold composting. Worms and other soil creatures will be doing most of the work. If, on the other hand, you want to speed things up, there are a number of simple things you can do if you're willing to be more involved. When you do them fairly consistently, you'll end up with a hot pile, where bacteria and soil microbes do the composting.

Hot Compost

You may have decided you want lots of compost and you want it now. The main difference between a hot pile and a cold pile is in the intervals between turning and moistening. The more you turn it and wet it down, the faster it works—it's that easy! A hot, active pile is actually hot. When you flip the material over, you can feel the heat (and sometimes even see it as steam). Worms and other visible composters can't live in this kind of environment, but microorganisms are busy composting for you.

Cold Compost

This method lets little soil creatures, ones you can actually see, do the work for you. Worms, centipedes, millipedes, springtails, pill bugs and even slugs are composters. Bacteria and soil microorganisms are also at work in a cold pile. You can let them do their work in a worm bin or in a pile in the yard. Just be sure to provide the three basic ingredients—waste, moisture, air, water. Turning it once a month is often enough to keep things from becoming anaerobic.

The Yard Waste Bin

Most compost bins are rectangular boxes with the back taller than the front so you can easily lean over and move the compost from one side to the other. One traditional design is the rectangular box divided into three sections. The first section is where the fresh stuff goes, the middle is half-composted, and the last one contains the near-ready or usable compost. When you move things from one area to the next, you also work air into the piles. Fancier models have hinged lids and removable fronts for easier turning.

If you do decide to build one, keep in mind that you want the pile to be accessible. You should be able to moisten and aerate it easily. Your bin could be as simple as four pallets lashed together or a round column of chicken wire. Just make sure you can undo them to get at the finished compost. If you're not interested in making one, there are manufactured bins at many nurseries and home improvement stores. Most of them are shaped like a covered canister with a little door that slides up from the ground so you can access your compost.

A WORM UTOPIA

Worms have specific needs. They like dark, damp, cool places. When you are composting with worms, you need to provide for their every whim so they can handily turn garbage into compost. Start with a rectangular box with a lid. Most worm bins are much smaller than a regular compost bin. They're usually made of wood, but if you're careful to punch drainage holes in the bottom, a large plastic storage tub will also do. It's critical to leave an avenue for excess moisture and heat to escape (stay away from clear plastic and select the darkest color possible). Worm bins are most successful when they're put in a protected environment (such as a garage, large shed, or under eaves), someplace where the contents won't freeze in the winter or cook in the summer.

In addition to the external structure of a bin, worms need an internal structure—a bedding medium—to live in. You can use newspaper and cardboard torn into strips, leaves, hay, or peat moss, to name a few possibilities. It's important that the medium be damp. Worms need mois-ture in order to breathe through their skins. The bedding medium should be organic and compostable, because the worms will also consume this along the way.

There is one right species of worm for the job. They are known by many names, but probably most commonly as red wigglers. You can find red wigglers sold as fishing bait. They're not the same as night crawlers, which won't sur-vive long in a worm bin. You may even have red wigglers already at work in your yard. Check piles of fallen leaves for the little guys.

After you've provided the bin, the bedding, and the worms, all that's needed is the garbage. Worm bins are most effective at transforming kitchen waste—fruit and vegetable peelings, leftover baked potatoes, bread crusts, etc. Add this food to the bin in small piles or zones. The worms will congregate, consume, and compost there. After one zone is nearly finished, start another. Your workforce will follow the food all around the box. When it looks as if you have more compost than bedding or waste, it's time to clean it out. Spread the contents in a thick layer on a tarp in bright light. Because worms abhor light, they will burrow as deep as possible. Scoop the good stuff off the top. Add any par-tially composted material to the new bedding in the bin, and put the worms back to work.

C. SUCCESS WITH SEEDS

Understanding how seeding occurs in nature serves as a model for successful outdoor seeding. In the late summer and early fall, seeds ripen in their pods. Then, by wind, birds, gravity—whatever means Mother Nature has at hand—they're randomly shaken from their pods and broadcast. The seeds hit the ground and sit there until seasonal rains and hospitable soil temperatures make germination possible.

ELIMINATE NATURE'S RANDOMNESS TO GET WHAT YOU WANT

1. First, get seeds, which is simple enough. You can mail order, shop retail, or collect straight from the plant. However, not all seeds will yield a plant with the same flower color they were collected from, as they revert to earlier lineage. In fact, some hybrid parents are sterile. If you've had problems in the past, the answer could be that simple. If you'd like to try harvesting your own seeds, wait until the pod has dried and changed color (usually brown, black, buff, etc.). Gently shake the pod. If you hear seeds rattling around, they're ready. If not, wait. Fresh seeds won't germinate. Remember, they'd have to be loose enough to fly out of the pod if they were being distributed naturally. You'll need envelopes, a large sheet of paper, and a cutting tool such as scissors or hand pruners. Carefully cut the branch,

carrying it upright to the paper. Shake the seeds out and use the paper as a funnel to get them into the envelope. Label the envelope!

2. Wait to seed until the air and soil have warmed in the spring, when the majority of plants have the highest likelihood of germination and survival. If you can stand gardening in a mist or light rain, you'll be working with Mother Nature. (Seeding in a torrential downpour won't work. Aren't you glad?) But not all plants need warm spring weather to germinate. In fact, a few actually favor late winter or early spring conditions, when the sun has warmed the soil, but air temperatures still fluctuate. Your clue for these seeds is the phrase "as soon as the soil warms" on the package. Still other plants can be seeded in the fall. Seed packets and catalogs usually note this, as will a good gardening book.

3. Dampen the soil, which can simply be a matter of waiting until a good rain has done the work for you.

4. Lightly loosen the soil with a hand rake. In order to know which seedlings are weeds and which are the ones you purposefully planted, seed in rows. You can always transplant them later in more random patterns. It's not important that the lines be parallel, just a pattern that you'll recognize later.

5. Sprinkle your seeds out of the package. If the seeds are very small, mix them with a pinch of sand to help distribute them more evenly. If the directions say they require a period of darkness to germinate, cover them with newspaper until they do. Large seeds, like those of sweet peas and nasturtiums, only

need to be pushed into the ground as deep as the seed is wide and barely covered.

6. Water. If you've opted to seed in dry weather, lightly mist frequently. Gushing water will wash away the seeds, but if you let them dry out, they won't germinate. They can perish quickly since they don't have deep roots to find moisture in the soil.

7. Thin out the seedlings, which is a hard thing to do after you've invested this much effort. But if you don't, they will choke each other out competing for sun, air, space, and water. A few strong plants are preferable to a mass of spindly ones. Packages have many seeds, so you can be picky about which plants will stay and which will be going. Ten strong, healthy plants for $1.29 isn't a bad investment.

D. FERTILIZER

LET'S START WITH THE NUMBERS

Simply put, those three numbers on the front of fertilizer containers pertain to the amounts of nitrogen, phosporus, and potassium in the formula. These three ingredients are principal plant nutrients. When the numbers are the same—12/12/12, or 20/20/20, or 6/6/6—your plants are receiving a well-balanced diet, and you can't go wrong with that.

Whenever there's a large disparity between the numbers (such as 33/11/11), that fertilizer has been formulated for a specific task (in this case a food for acid-loving plants such as azaleas). Labels tell you which plants the formula is for and how to use the food correctly, but a little nutrient savvy can help you make sure you get what you need.

Nitrogen (N) does lots of things, but most importantly, it keeps plants green and growing. Without enough nitrogen, plants have yellow stunted leaves. With too much they develop weak, soft growth susceptible to breakage and frost damage. An example of a fertilizer formula high in nitrogen is 40/4/4, sold as lawn food.

Phosphorous (P) is essential for root development, disease resistance, and seed and fruit formation. When there is a phosphorous deficiency, plants stop maturing; they're stunted, with purplish-red stems and leaves. Fertilizers promoted as bloom enhancers are often high in phosphorous and potash.

Potash (potassium) (K) aids disease resistance and helps harden tender shoots, protecting plants from desiccation when the weather is extremely cold or dry. It also contributes to the formation of strong flowers and fruits. You'll know your plants are deficient when leaf edges and tips look scorched with yellow streaks and when flower and fruit production is poor.

DELIVERING THE GOODS TO YOUR PLANTS VIA CHEMICALS

COATED GRANULES AND SPIKES

Advantages. Coated granules are easy to distribute around plants, and provide nourishment evenly to root systems. Applied once, usually in early spring when most people are eagerly out gardening, they put fertilizer in the soil without further effort from you. Granules are mixed into the soil and spikes are usually pushed or hammered in, depending on their size. As the weather warms, both spikes and coated granules release nutrients. Both types can be used in conjunction with diluted liquid fertilizers.

Disadvantages. Of the chemical fertilizers, coated granules usually cost the most. They're not effective during cool weather and only work for a limited time. Although spikes are more reasonably priced, you'll need plenty of them around larger plants and trees because they concentrate fertilizer in their immediate vicinity.

CONCENTRATED LIQUIDS

Advantages. Concentrated liquids are less expensive than coated granules and spikes. If you use a hose-end sprayer, you can take the guessing out of mixing and easily cover a large area in short order. With sprayed fertilizer, plants receive the benefits immediately by taking it in through their leaves (called foliar feeding). Plus, you'll be getting two chores done at once, watering and fertilizing.

Disadvantages. Care must be taken when spraying. Spraying water over plants prone to mildew (such as roses) tends to exacerbate the problem, so you'll have to spray around the base of those plants instead. You can scorch the leaves if you apply fertilizer in hot weather or during the heat of midday. Also, a once-a-season application is not enough if you want these fertilizers to do their job.

Dry Granular

Advantages. For feeding roses, dry granular fertilizer is the best way to go. You can avoid spreading mildew, blackspot, and rust by carefully watering only the soil directly around the plant base. Your roses get a nice deep soak, from which they benefit immensely. Many granular rose foods include a systemic insect repellent; it's taken up through the stem, killing only the insects directly feeding on the plant. Thus you avoid applying a blanket insecticide over nearby healthy plants. For all other plants, the only real advantage of dry granular fertilizer is the low price, because it'll take more work than the previously described fertilizers.

Disadvantages. Granular fertilizers must be scratched into damp soil to dissolve and release the nutrients. (Don't confuse them with coated granules, which rely on warm soil temperatures and watering to dissolve the coating before releasing any food.) So you end up watering twice— once to get the soil wet before you apply the fertilizer and again to help the roots begin taking up nutrients. If you don't do this, you're wasting your time and money because the granules just end up sitting there and your plants can't benefit.

DELIVERING THE GOODS TO YOUR PLANTS ORGANICALLY

ANIMAL MANURES AND COMPOST

Advantages. Manure and compost work well as soil conditioners, mulches, and fertilizers. They are not used primarily as a fertilizer, although they do contain some nutrients. If you happen to be a composter, purposefully adding varied ingredients such as eggshells, orange skins, coffee grounds, and bone meal will improve the nutrient content.

Disadvantages. Manure and compost are smelly, bulky, and require sweat investment to distribute over your beds. Manure fresh from the farm will "burn" your plants while decomposing, so be sure to let it break down before you use it in your garden. Decomposition happens faster in summer. Dump it in a place in your yard where it won't bother you, and turn it as you would compost until it doesn't clump together or resemble what it was originally, and the smell dissipates. It should be crumbly, dark, and dry.

FISH EMULSIONS

Advantages. Some people absolutely swear by fish fertilizers, even going so far as to bury dead fish in their gardens. Fish fertilizer does have a well-deserved reputation as plant food.

Disadvantages. Fish fertilizer can try neighborhood relationships if the smelly variety is used on a regular basis in large quantities. There are deodorized versions available in liquid and pellet forms. Fish fertilizer is laborious to hand mix and impossible to use in a hose-end sprayer.

Blood Meal and Bone Meal

Advantages. Blood meal and bone meal are high in nitrogen.

Disadvantages. Because they are attractive to dogs and other animals, it's best to work them into the soil immediately. Also, blood meal and bone meal are relatively expensive, so it's more cost-effective to work them in around specific shrubs rather than broadcasting them over your flower beds, as they add no benefit, such as soil conditioning.

Index